MW01121699

Labours
of
Love

Labours
of Love

Canadians Talk About Adoption

Deborah A. Brennan

DUNDURN PRESS
TORONTO

Copyright © **Deborah A. Brennan**, 2008

All rights reserved. No part of this publication may be reproduced, stored in a retrieval system, or transmitted in any form or by any means, electronic, mechanical, photocopying, recording, or otherwise (except for brief passages for purposes of review) without the prior permission of Dundurn Press. Permission to photocopy should be requested from Access Copyright.

Copy-editor: Andrea Waters
Designer: Jennifer Scott
Printer: Marquis

Library and Archives Canada Cataloguing in Publication

Brennan, Deborah A.
        Labours of love : Canadians talk about adoption / by Deborah A. Brennan.

ISBN 978-1-55002-845-4

1. Adoption--Canada. 2. Adoptive parents--Canada. 3. Parenting--Canada. I. Title.

HV875.7.C3B74 2008   362.7340971   C2008-904875-X

1   2   3   4   5   12   11   10   09   08

Conseil des Arts du Canada   Canada Council for the Arts   Canadä   ONTARIO ARTS COUNCIL CONSEIL DES ARTS DE L'ONTARIO

We acknowledge the support of the **Canada Council for the Arts** and the **Ontario Arts Council** for our publishing program. We also acknowledge the financial support of the **Government of Canada** through the **Book Publishing Industry Development Program** and **The Association for the Export of Canadian Books**, and the **Government of Ontario** through the **Ontario Book Publishers Tax Credit** program and the **Ontario Media Development Corporation**.

Care has been taken to trace the ownership of copyright material used in this book. The author and the publisher welcome any information enabling them to rectify any references or credits in subsequent editions.

J. Kirk Howard, President

Printed and bound in Canada
www.dundurn.com

Dundurn Press
3 Church Street, Suite 500
Toronto, Ontario, Canada
M5E 1M2

Gazelle Book Services Limited
White Cross Mills
High Town, Lancaster, England
LA1 4XS

Dundurn Press
2250 Military Road
Tonawanda, NY U.S.A.
14150

For Diana
Whose presence in our lives gives us infinite joy and never-ending adventures

And for Artrina
Who entrusted us with her care

Table ^{of}Contents

Foreword

Sandra Scarth
Bachelor of Social Work
President, Adoption Council of Canada
Adoptive Mother

TO THE WONDERFUL families who shared their stories.

This book is a welcome addition to adoption literature in Canada. It was never intended to be a comprehensive text on adoption; rather, it is truly a labour of love by an adoptive parent who feels there is a gap in the information about adoption available to adoptive parents and the public. There are how-to books or guides for adoptive parents, but some are negative and few examine the impact of the process on adoptive parents, adoptees, and their extended families, both birth and adoptive. Yet the way everyone involved in an adoption feels about it influences the decisions that must be made and profoundly affects the outcome.

The first and largest part of the book is a series of informal conversations with a diverse group of adoptive parents, birthparents, and adopted children who share very personal feelings about their experiences. Despite the stress that some of the adoptive parents experienced with infertility issues and seemingly unending application and preparation processes, the overwhelming sense is that the joy of having created a family through adoption has more than compensated for their difficulties. Particularly compelling are the stories of families who have adopted children with challenges many of us would find overwhelming, yet they have persevered and helped the children to feel good about themselves.

Another theme that emerges early in the book is the understanding by most parents interviewed that maintaining a healthy relationship with birthparents is in the best interests of their children. This would not have been the case a few decades ago and points to the successful advocacy of adult adoptees and birthparents for more openness. Most of the stories describe very positive relationships between the birth and adoptive parents, and in several instances there is active involvement by the children. The birthparents acknowledge the pain most of them experienced but focus more on the satisfaction they feel because of their connection with the adoptive family, who keeps them informed about how their children are doing. What comes across is a sense of mutual respect that honours each of their roles.

The majority of the adoptees interviewed were in their teens or younger, and to this point in their lives they appear comfortable with their adoptions and the level of openness. Two older adoptees, a brother and sister adopted in the early 1970s in closed adoptions typical of the time, are candid about their current attempts to deal with the impact of their adoptions. Steve, adopted at five months, has felt disconnected to his parents and is now actively working out a better relationship with his adoptive mother. Christine finds that becoming a mother has given her greater empathy towards her birthmother. Neither is yet interested in meeting their birthparents.

The second part of the book is a series of interviews with professionals in the adoption community, many of whom have a personal connection to adoption as well. Pat Fenton talks about the need for more specialized training for adoption professionals. Brenda McCreight underscores the need for post-adoption supports, particularly respite for children who present behavioural challenges. Michael Grand eloquently outlines the issues around open records, noting the lag in public and political understanding of the positive outcomes in countries that have had open records for decades.

The author set out to write a book that celebrates the successes in adoption to offset the often negative stereotyping. I think she has succeeded. She has created a book that will be of value not only to those thinking about adoption but also to all those touched by adoption who want a better understanding of its effects on everyone involved. Adoption social workers and others concerned with adoption in their professional lives will also learn from listening to the wisdom of those living the experience.

Introduction

MY FIRST NOTION about writing this book came at the beginning of our adoption journey, while I was scouring bookstores in an effort to find adoption resources. I could find only one that dealt with Canada. It was *The Canadian Adoption Guide — A Family at Last*, by Judith Wine. The book gave us practical advice on navigating the process, but little about the experience afterwards. Many of the other books I found were difficult to read beyond a few chapters. They were full of negative "what ifs" about the potentially insurmountable challenges in adoption. Needless to say, quite a few of these books are still gathering dust on my shelves.

When my husband and I began actively pursuing adoption, we were again met with predictions of a doubtful positive outcome, particularly because we wanted to adopt domestically and because the small details of being over forty and having a biological son would be perceived by potential birthparents as disadvantages. In some ways it was to my benefit that I didn't read too much or talk to many others about it, as I might have quit before even beginning!

For some still inexplicable reason, I forged ahead with blinders on, determined to prove the naysayers wrong. In the ensuing months I learned that quiet, well-planned, and unrelenting perseverance in one's goal to parent through adoption is essential. There will be a myriad of challenges, heartaches, and uncertainties that will test your endurance along the way. I also learned that all of this is completely necessary and that, as with the most uncomfortable of pregnancies and labours, when that part is over and your child is in your arms, the rest becomes a distant memory.

The most surprising aspect of our adoption experience throughout has been the lack of basic understanding about adoption in Canada from both a practical and a social perspective. I have come to believe, because of personal experience, that the word *adoption* automatically triggers flashes of negativity for many people. It's almost as if they think that the circumstances necessitating adoption are always the result of something bad happening. While it is true that adoption can be a result of very difficult, sometimes abusive or neglectful circumstances, that should not colour our view of the children. The circumstances surrounding adoptions should be acknowledged and taken into account in the life of the adoptee, not submerged under the desires of well-intentioned parents. Somehow they think that by loving their children enough and shielding them from the truth of their origins, denying them an emotional connection to their birth families, everything will be just fine. Not necessarily so.

The subject of adoption, like religion or politics, is able to ignite heated and passionate debates. How we think about adoption is deeply rooted in how our parents thought about it. Most of those who were not personally affected by it didn't give it any thought at all. And although my research conservatively says that one in five Canadians have had personal experience in adoption as birthparents, adoptees, or adoptive parents, it is still a subject that stays in a protected subculture of society. The media loves to report on sensational celebrity adoptions or adoptions gone wrong — but what about those in the majority? We need to hear more about the successes, about the families who, through adversity, illustrate love, patience, and a willingness to, as Cathy Gilbert says, be there for the long haul. The acknowledgement of and respect towards adoptees' birth families is essential. How else can they make sense of their place in the world? Some people may ask, What if the story of their origins involves painful realities? Surely we must not reveal those truths? Michael Grand, psychology professor at the University of Guelph, believes that the worst stories are the ones that are never told. It is in the telling that we can begin to heal.

The stories within the pages of *Labours of Love* are all variations on a central theme that rises high above any stigma that still exists surrounding adoption: Families, however they are created, are to be celebrated and embraced by us all. I feel honoured to have spent time with every one of them as I travelled across Canada to be welcomed into their homes. We shared laughter, tears, and an unequivocal sense that the children we have the privilege of loving are meant to be with us. While the book offers glimpses into the lives of a few very special families, I met so many others along the way who, when hearing about this project, were anxious to tell me their stories ... from seatmates on airplanes to grocery checkout clerks to bed and breakfast owners. Everyone was interested in sharing how adoption has touched their lives. My hope is that the words spoken and images seen in *Labours of Love* will open a door to honest and respectful dialogue about a topic that affects many but is still understood by few. The misconceptions about adoption can easily be erased if we are open to listening. With knowledge and understanding come empathy and compassion. Listen to the voices of experience in *Labours of Love*, for they have much to teach us.

The
Families

If a child is raised in a home that is loving and nurturing, where there is complete truth about who you are, you can't give a child any greater place from which to fly.
— Amanda Bearse, adoptive parent

Photo by Liz Lott.

Photo by Rebecca Craigie.

Raising children is like making biscuits: it's as easy to raise a big batch as one, while you have your hands in the dough.

E.W. Howe

Paying it Forward
The Gilbert Family
Nanaimo, British Columbia

"He stamped me with a belief in justice, then drenched me in culpability."
— Barbara Kingsolver, *The Poisonwood Bible*

I LOVE THE West Coast of Canada. There are some things about it that are almost predictable — like it will probably be raining when you go, but the people you will meet really value the quality of life, so the rain won't matter. And when the skies clear, the spectacular scenery that emerges will make you forget it ever was raining.

My anticipation at meeting the Gilbert family in Nanaimo is overshadowed by my feelings of dread as I step onto a float plane for the flight to Vancouver Island. The rain has been steady all day, and accompanying it is thick, "cut it with a knife" fog that leaves the visibility at nil. The fellow flying the rickety old plane looks about eighteen, but he brightly reassures me, as he stubs out his cigarette, that because the ceiling is so low we'll be flying very close to the water. *Good*, I think, *at least if we collide with another plane or some sort of sea bird we'll float — won't we?*

The reason I am so excited to meet the Gilberts is because they are the parents of fifteen children — four biological and eleven adopted. I simply cannot fathom it, but I am about to spend the next twenty-four hours experiencing it for myself.

Cathy and Dave Gilbert meet me at the float plane dock right on time, and I smile as if I am a pro at this, while attempting to regain the strength in my wobbly legs. They announce that we are going for lunch, and soon I find myself at a table in front of a blazing fire in one of their favourite restaurants. I like them immediately. They look normal, act normal, and even have a great sense of humour. How could a couple with fifteen children be so normal? They are not — they are extraordinary. Over lunch I see the first indications of that in this amazing duo.

Cathy confesses, "Our life from the beginning has been a little nutty. We met in 1978 when we were nineteen, were engaged five weeks later, and married in six months. We felt completely in sync with one another and to this day are each other's best friend. When our first child, Jenny, was two months old, we crammed everything and ourselves into an old Ford Comet and drove to B.C."

Both Cathy and Dave grew up in families that influenced them in terms of social responsibility. Dave was the son of an Anglican minister, a profession he almost pursued himself. Cathy spent time in Africa with Canada World Youth and L'Arche, and Dave went with the Anglican Church on a co-op exposure trip to Mexico to see first-hand the realities of poverty.

It was after this trip in 1989 that Cathy and Dave became serious about adopting. In the beginning of her search, Cathy found the Ministry of Children and Family Development in British Columbia discouraging, because of concerns regarding birth order and their biological children. In the fall of that year, the Gilberts did some respite care for two children in foster care who went back and forth from their birthparents to care for years (when Cathy saw them again ten years later they still had not been adopted).

Cathy: "I found this so sad, that they had been bounced around all those years. It really solidified for us that what we wanted to do was the right thing. When we first applied to adopt, our daughter Maggie was two. After almost three years of nothing happening we decided to try to have another baby, when our social worker [with whom they worked from 1988 to 2000] called."

Usually adoptions don't take place when a potential adoptive mother is pregnant, but in the Gilberts' case, their first adoption, of four-year-old Carl in 1991, would be the beginning of a pattern of determined advocacy on Cathy's part. This became something of an education for all the adoption professionals fortunate enough to cross their paths in the following years.

Baby Dorothy was born in March, to be welcomed by her three biological siblings and new brother Carl, who had moved in three months prior.

Cathy: "A year later we reapplied with a view to adopting an older child, but readjusted our 'no more babies' mindset to welcome twelve-day-old Rachel to the family in 1993. When Rachel was one, we reapplied again and heard about twelve-year-old Richard. Richard had lived in fourteen foster homes and had suffered emotional and physical abuses. One of the most significant things in Richard's life in foster care had been a desire to play team sports. He had been told over and over again that once he was adopted he could play hockey and other sports (since he would be in a home long enough to play for a whole season!). He moved in with this vision … and play he did. Hockey, baseball, rugby, football — he played them all; making up for lost time, it would seem."

The Gilberts' biological son, William, was the same age as Richard when he joined the family in 1995, and in retrospect they feel it was quite hard on William. When the family moved to Vancouver Island in 2000, William chose to stay on the mainland. Cathy originally wondered how he felt about the adoption of Richard, since they were so close in age, but William has since said to her, "It made me who I am; and if you like who I am, I guess you did the right thing." (William lives in Ladner with his fiancée and eleven-month-old baby boy. He works in construction and renovation.)

Cathy and Dave's fourth adoption, of Carl's ten-year-old biological sibling, Alex, was a little more of a challenge. They learned that the ministry was considering not placing him with them. Cathy went above the worker's head and wrote a strong letter to the area manager of the ministry. She asked how they could possibly have a better plan for Alex than to place him with his biological brother? Just to make sure the bases were completely covered, Cathy also phoned the office to speak to Alex's worker. Cathy said, "I understand you've made a decision not to place Alex with us — I'd like to speak to the supervisor, please." To which the woman replied, "I *am* the supervisor." Needless to say, Alex joined his brother as the fourth adopted addition to the Gilbert family in 1996 (that made eight, in case you were losing track).

By this time, Cathy had become quite adept at navigating the system in British Columbia and was becoming known to the adoption community. She and Dave were attending an

Adoption Awareness Christmas party in 2000 when a worker looked at a nine-year-old boy named Raymond and said, "See that kid over there? His adoption has broken down; would you consider adopting him?"

Cathy: "I was trying not to look at him, but of course I did. Our daughter Dorothy, who was with us that day, was about the same age as Ray, and to this day is very astute. When we left, Dave and I sat in the front trying to talk in code about the possibility of adopting this boy. When we got out of the car, Dorothy nonchalantly asked, 'So are we going to adopt him?'"

Eight months later, in the summer of 2001, Raymond joined the family. Raymond had recently lived in an-all female household and had a perception that girls always got him in trouble; the Gilberts learned that they had to be fair about discipline so his outlook on girls would become more positive. Their efforts helped, because today Raymond and Dorothy are very close.

The Gilberts' next adoption came about after Cathy made an inquiry about some children she'd heard about who were in foster care and awaiting an adoptive family. The social worker immediately said to Cathy, "Are you thinking of adopting again? Let me show you a video of some children who really need a family."

Cathy: "I took the video home, Dave and I watched it, and of course that was it. Sarah was nine and Jessie seven when the adoption plans that were being made for them fell through. Jessie has since been diagnosed with Autism Spectrum Disorder, and both had been abused and neglected as small children, but like all the Gilbert adoptions, it wasn't long before it seemed they had been there forever shortly after they came to us in 2002." (Now we are at eleven.)

About a year later the Gilberts heard about another situation that touched their hearts. Cathy remembers talking with Dave about it as they went up and down the aisles of Costco. It was another adoption breakdown involving three children: two boys, six and nine, and a four-year-old girl. There had been a month of pre-placement visits followed by a short placement with the potential adoptive parents, who then decided they could not parent the children, so they were sent back to foster care. There was a limited time frame, so the Gilberts met with the children's psychiatrist, only to hear information that horrified them. The two boys,

Dalton and Chris, were on medications including Ritalin, antidepressants, an antipsychotic, and sleep medication. There was a paper trail of frequent moves and reports of challenging behaviour. The little girl, Liean, by all accounts seemed be to developing typically.

Cathy: "When we met the children it was disturbing. They came to us immediately and called us Mom and Dad, got on our laps, and showed many signs that to the untrained would look like attachment but were actually the opposite. The psychiatrist said to us, 'What makes you think you can do this?' and tried to get us to commit to keeping them on their medication, saying, 'You're not going to change their meds, are you?'"

Dave: "Chris was more medicated than Dalton — so much so that he had facial tics and was just a quivering mass of nerves."

Cathy: "When they came home, all hell broke loose. Liean wanted to be carried all the time, and there was constant defiance from the boys. It was a pretty stressful period in our lives while we adjusted to three new children trying to connect with us in this zoo. We took them to our pediatrician to wean them off the medications. He had faith in our parenting skills and said to us, 'Either that psychiatrist is crazy or you're crazy, and I am betting on the psychiatrist.' Chris and Dalton are now completely medication-free."

Cathy heard about their most recent adoption through their network in the adoption community, who by then knew their family well. A child who had come to Canada from Texas was going to be returned there due to an adoption disruption. "I called Dave, who was in his car driving in Vancouver, to discuss the idea, and he had to pull over," Cathy recalls. Seven-year-old Marcus was in the private adoption system, and his adoption had to be facilitated by a judge in Texas. When the time came for finalization, Dave was on a ship off the coast of Oregon.

Cathy: "In June of 2007, I went to the courthouse in Nanaimo with Marcus while Dave was on a satellite phone, with the ship's captain verifying his identity with the judge."

Dave: "I had to do all the swearing in over the phone. It was quite something. The judge proclaimed in his Texas drawl, 'I've never done one like that before!'"

Cathy: "Because of the adoption disruption, I am sure Marcus didn't trust the words of the adults in his life. But while we were in court he got to hear me assuring the judge, the social worker, and the lawyer that I loved him with all my heart (after swearing in on a Bible!). I think that had an impact and was part of the healing and beginning of trust in us as his parents. It was a very special day."

Marcus had a rough first year and didn't do well at school, but he has flourished in his second. He is making great progress in his development.

Cathy: "He had been used to frequent moves and a pretty negative environment, and never expected anything to go well. We've used a reward system with his teachers for consistently good behaviour. He needs to be reassured that we're here to love and help him now — for good, this time."

We have been sitting in the Gilberts' living room while they describe the sequence of their children's adoptions. Each child they have adopted has some level of special need in varying degrees, including Autism Spectrum Disorder, Fetal Alcohol Spectrum Disorder, Attention Deficit Hyperactive Disorder, Neonatal Abstinence Syndrome, and learning disabilities. Some have suffered abuse, neglect, and abandonment, and all deal with trust issues.

As we are winding up our discussion, twenty-four-year-old Richard arrives with his fiancée, Kayla, and baby boy, Dylan. They live in Nanaimo and have come for dinner and for Richard to tell me about life with the Gilberts in the last twelve years. Before we can manage to head off to a quiet spot to talk, the rest of the Gilberts arrive home from school, or in Carl's case, from his job, and I meet each one by one, thinking, *Where are the name tags?* I fully expect chaos to ensue, and perhaps the children are on their best behaviour, but after chatting about their day and formally introducing me to their three dogs, Rufus, Hoover, and

Photo by Rebecca Craigie.

(clockwise from front left) Cathy, Liean, Jenny, Maggie, Rachel, Dorothy, Sarah, William, Carl, Richard, Ray, Alex, Jessie, Dalton, Chris, Marcus, Dave.

Murphy, their two rats, Simon and Garfunkel, and two cats, Spike and Tigger, everyone drifts away to engage in various activities. *Wait till dinner*, I think to myself, *then we'll see!*

I ask Richard to share his recollections about his adoption.

Richard: "I remember everything from the beginning. I was in fourteen foster homes, all on the mainland. The last one was in Surrey, and I was there for two years. I had become very attached to my foster parents, so when they said there was a great family who wanted to meet me, I had mixed feelings. I said I wanted a big family, not thinking that it would end up being one this big! The first time I met the family, I met everyone. I was excited when they came to the foster home, but nervous, and I asked William lots of questions about his friends and school. Everyone was friendly and warm, and they showed me lots of pictures of their family life. I thought they were awesome.

"I saw the house once before I moved in, and they showed me where my room was and said I could put some pictures up. It was hard to leave my foster home, I didn't want to cry, but I did, and Mom cried too when she came to pick me up. It was good. There was a big banner up that said, 'Welcome Home Richard.'

"I had another life to get used to: school, church, new friends — everyone was great. Carl and Rachel had been adopted before me, and then Alex came. Every year there seemed to be someone else coming, but it was fine for me. I was busy in high school, and having all the kids never made my relationship with my parents any less. They still came to all my games and never left me behind."

I ask Richard if he remembers his birthmother. "I remember my biological mother and have pictures of her," he says. "When we moved to the island in 2000, I lost track of her, but her best friend recently told me that she's doing good."

Richard shares how having a child of his own has changed his perspective about being adopted.

Richard: "It definitely has changed how I feel about adoption. Every day I think about how I will take care of my son. I never want him to go through what I went through. I'm always going to be there for him. I don't know how you can have a child and just leave him. I have friends who have had bad upbringings. I don't dwell on the past, and don't see why I should be an angry kid. I do have a family — I'm lucky; everything is good. I don't see why I should go cause trouble."

Even though Richard has started a new life away from the family home, he still spends as much time as he can with them. "I'm so happy to see my parents and my brothers and sisters. I want to keep that bond. I've been able to create strong relationships with the kids. My parents are great — they've always been there for me. Their parenting and discipline is a very good example for me now with my son."

In addition to speaking with Richard, the couple's eldest adopted son, I am able to talk with their eldest biological daughter, who has some very interesting perspectives to share. Jenny, twenty-seven, is living in Toronto and working on a master's degree in religion. Jenny was eleven when her parents adopted Carl, the first child in what she termed an adoption avalanche: the children just kept on coming.

Jenny: "In the beginning I was glad that my parents chose to adopt, because we had fostered a girl, and it was traumatic for me when she left. My memories of Carl are that he was difficult to care for; he wouldn't eat and required a lot of focused attention. But seeing Carl today is amazing. He moved out after high school and has been working steadily at a fibreglass shop: living on his own and sustaining a full-time job are successes that we weren't sure were going to be possible for him. He's contributing in a meaningful way. I remember the day Rachel was born we were supposed to go to the water park, and of course we didn't — I was very disappointed, but also excited! Rachel was a not an easy baby, though, which was obviously difficult for everyone. By the time Richard came, I was fifteen and in high school. He and my brother William had some conflicts around friends, and I found as I went on through high school, it was the most difficult time for me and my parents. They were dealing with all kinds of things with all the kids. The most difficult aspect of having such a large family was that sometimes I felt I wasn't getting the attention I needed."

Jenny left home when she was seventeen and attended an alternative high school in Vancouver. She also spent time in Ecuador with Canada World Youth. I ask her if she sometimes felt a burden of responsibility, being the eldest child in such a large family.

"Yes, definitely; I often felt like parent number three. I was asked to babysit a lot, and though I must say that my parents always made a point of paying me for my efforts, I often felt that it was an obligation, despite the fact that it was framed as a choice. My parents always made an effort, however, to spend time with us four older kids by taking us skiing or out to dinner, but there were definitely times when I felt I wasn't getting enough one-on-one time with my parents."

Jenny is very concerned that her comments are sounding too negative, and I say they sound completely normal based on her experiences. I tell her that if she didn't feel these things I would be surprised.

Now as an adult, and having lived independently for quite some time, she can look at things more objectively.

Jenny: "It's interesting that whenever I talk about my family, everyone says, 'Your parents are so amazing,' and it makes me gag a bit. They're just my parents — they've made choices that maybe I wouldn't make. The thing is, I know why they are amazing. They have no expectations for getting anything back. A lot of the kids are hard to love, hard to like … some may grow up and might say they could have done better. My parents put their hearts and souls into taking care of them every day.

"My parents are selfless people. They have taught us a lot about helping others. They don't just talk about it, they do it. They have taught us all to be socially conscious, to be sympathetic to those who have less, and to care about the world. At Christmas the kids pick a charity and help make a Christmas dinner for families who might otherwise not have one. I remember my mother telling me about a situation involving the kids and one of their friends. The other boy was telling them about getting his new shoes at a popular big box store. Raymond said, 'We don't shop there. Don't you know that they are the biggest sweatshop employer in the world?' So I can see the positive influences my parents have had on all of us. On any given day when they see one of the kids show progress, it makes them feel good, not good for themselves but good for the kid.

"My whole life I always admired my parents' relationship, and I want that for myself. They are each other's best friend — they are on the same page. They could not have done this if they had not been. They've instilled in me a desire to live my life doing something that has a value to our society. For my parents, it is helping children. People look at the enormity of the problems in the world and wonder what they can do. When you parent a child who can ultimately make a contribution, and who might otherwise take a negative path, you have played an essential part in the success of the child — and that is enough."

When we return to the living room, the kitchen is a hive of activity with dinner preparations, and the dining hall–style table is set. Cathy is preparing vegetables with the help of Marcus and Alex; Dave is finishing off the main course and dessert. We all sit down together at the bountiful feast, join hands, and give thanks. Cathy holds court at

Photo by Rebecca Craigie.

Dinner is always a shared effort. This night, Alex, Chris, and Marcus help Mom out.

one end of the table, Dave at the other, and within minutes we all are happily eating and chatting. No one is whining, crying, or throwing food. Everyone is eating the same thing and quite happily so. "You don't do this kind of dinner every night of the week, do you?" I ask. Cathy and Dave look up at me with puzzled looks and answer, "Well, yes — pretty much."

Both before and after dinner, I offer my assistance and am encouraged to relax as everything is under control. Indeed it is. I remain at the table and invite the kids to sit with me for a chat. I ask them to share what the best things are about being adopted by the Gilberts and about being a part of such a big family. Most are eager to tell me.

Jessie (age twelve): "There's always someone to talk to and share feelings with; you're never alone."

Chris (age ten): "There's always someone to look up to and ask for help. I was adopted when I was six, and it feels like I've always been here. I feel safe and secure. We have a really big house, a good school, and I really like the food here."

Alex (age sixteen): "When I got hit by the car, they took care of me really well, and I had lots of visits from my brothers and sisters. You get good hand-me-down clothes; we're just a normal family except that it's big."

Sarah (age fourteen): "I remember when Jessie and I were adopted — I was nine. We were happy. Finally, you can have a place and it's yours forever. Nobody can take that away from you."

Rachel (age fourteen): "I was twelve days old when I was adopted. When Sarah came, it was amazing. When we moved to the island we got a room together. We're teenage girls, but we're very different; I'm the tough one."

Jessie: "Being adopted is good. You don't have a social worker and you don't have to switch families all the time. They keep you — but you can get into trouble. I can be very bad and they'll still love me."

Marcus: "I'm eight. I have lots of brothers and sisters and they treat me well."

Liean: "I'm eight and I'm in Grade 3. Being adopted is okay. It was scary at first, but then I got used to it. When I get hurt, I have lots of sisters and brothers that ask me what happened and then help me. I have my own swing and sandbox and I climb trees. When I go to bed, I have my Dora blanket that I sleep with every night. I go to bed at night feeling happy."

Dalton: "I'm thirteen, and what I know is that being adopted means you have a family who takes you in, takes care of you, gives you a home, and treats you like you were their own. We do fun stuff like boat trips. For foster care you live with people who just look after you and you don't call them Mom and Dad; you call them by their first names. When you get adopted you know it's forever and you're never moving again."

Jessie: "When you have older siblings you can tackle them and they won't cry. They help you build stuff. Sometimes working together is hard. We have fights and tattle on each other. I don't know how Mom and Dad do it. They must have magic powers."

So that explains it — well, partly anyway. Of course, even with the patience, organizational skills, and sheer energy it takes to raise fifteen children, the Gilberts have had more than their share of personal setbacks. Cathy lost her mother to lung cancer in 1988; Cathy's father and Dave's father died in 2001; and in 2005, the unthinkable happened. Cathy recounts the accident that turned their family upside down.

Cathy: "When Alex was fourteen, he was hit by a car at the end of our driveway while he was riding his bike. Aside from the horror of it all — being in a coma for three weeks and in hospital for four months — it was a revelation to us, facing peoples' reactions and attitudes. While he was lying there on the side of the road, the paramedics and others kept asking if some-one had told a family member, not thinking that we were his family because he doesn't look like us. Also, what kept happening was people asked if it was one of our adopted kids, as if that would make a difference in the magnitude of our grief and worry! His accident was a brutal reminder that no matter what you plan, you're not always in control; not that you shouldn't live with a sense of purpose, but you have to live in the present and respond as best you can to it."

I ask the couple the questions that everyone must wonder — why they have done it, how they have done it, and, lastly, how their efforts reaffirm that their decisions have been the right ones for the family.

Cathy: "We both have a strong sense that this was meant to be; they're here for a reason. In the beginning we read a lot, went to some support groups and workshops, and talked to each other constantly. We were also fortunate to become friends with Brenda McCreight, who not only is an adoptive parent of twelve children considered to have special needs but also is a therapist whose expertise is child development and adoption-related issues. We discovered that consistency and predictability are key components. These kids need to know what's going to happen next, even if it's a good thing, and to know they are not going anywhere. We are here for the long haul. But how can they believe that when they've had so many years of other people being in control of you and telling you where you're going to live next? I don't know how they ever recovered, and I also know that we as parents can easily sabotage any progress simply by how we speak to them and how we react to behavioural challenges."

Cathy has an early childhood education background and special needs experience, and with Dave's complete and unwavering support, they have travelled this road together.

Cathy: "Dave never said no — never hesitated for an instant. The only practical thing he would ask would be, 'Where will they sleep?' to which I would respond, 'That's a minor detail.' Dave spent a lot of time in the beginning staying home with the kids while I worked full-time, but after Alex's accident we decided to switch positions. I'd only been at home for a week when I realized how hard it was!"

I ask the couple how much outside help they have had over the years.

Cathy: "We have tried to be as independent as possible and rely on each other, but of course we have had some family members, like my sister, helping out, especially after Alex's accident. I have learned to reach out more, especially when Dave's been away working."

In terms of social and physical supports for the children, Cathy has been a true advocate for each child's specific needs: emotional, academic, or otherwise. I get the sense that she has an extraordinary gift for focusing on their individual personalities. She recognizes what they need and wastes no time seeking out the appropriate help and resources, if they are available. But she tells me there's not enough post-adoption support, or the right kinds of support.

Cathy: "The system goes overboard telling people what can go wrong with adoptions of kids in foster care, in order to protect themselves. Instead, they need to capture people with an image of the kids that's not too scary, educate them about what that might look like, and then give them a lot of support along the way. The system has to say, 'Okay, you've done something risky and challenging, and your kid's going to need a lot of support and so are you, and you can do it!' People aren't hearing the right stuff and getting the supports to help them be successful. Ultimately, that's what leads to adoption breakdowns.

"I also think people really need to know themselves, what their own expectations are, and where they draw their own line in the sand. If you want to put your kids in a box, you shouldn't adopt, especially older children. People have to get to their own unresolved issues themselves before they can take on a child's."

Dave: "Some people that look into adoption are more concerned about the home study, the wait, the work of it all, and not about the kids that need them. We drove the process ourselves, but many don't have the wherewithal to do it — they don't know how. They expect the social workers to always come to them, but the system is crippled and there aren't enough bodies to drive it, let alone fix it. People need to be very proactive."

Cathy: "There are indications that international adoptions [certainly China] will take longer, and perhaps will become even more costly. We need to get the word out about all the kids here and then provide all the education, coping skills, and support that people need to stay in it for the long haul. I remember speaking one time at an adoption event, and Tom Christensen, the Minister for Children and Families, being moved to tears as I spoke about our son Richard. Hearing me talk about his significant progress made it real for him, and he rightly said, 'We can effect change in the next generation by what we do now.'"

The couple share some memories that illustrate that the love and commitment they have for their children is unwavering, however long it takes for them to believe it.

Dave: "One day I was making bows and arrows for the boys and Dalton said to me, 'Can I take this with me when I go?' I said, 'Where are you going?' and he said, 'Oh yeah, I'm not going anywhere, am I?' Dalton had been with us for a year and still had not grasped his permanent place in our family."

Cathy: "Raymond came to us when he was nine and had significant learning delays. He is fifteen now and has asked to read some of his reports from the psychologist. One day he was asking Lian [age eight] to name all the colours, and she rhymed them all off effortlessly.

Raymond said, 'When I was eight the only colour I knew was yellow — why would anyone adopt a kid like me?' After six years in our family he is realizing that we are those people, and that he is here to stay. Recently we planned to go away for a weekend with the kids, but Raymond wanted to stay back at a friend's instead. He came up to me and gave me a huge hug and said, 'I'm filled with torment.' I asked him, 'Are you filled with torment because you don't want to hurt our feelings by staying back with your friend?' We talked about it, and he ended up staying with his friend. This was a milestone for him, because to me it said he has developed a conscience and that his choices impact others. This is success."

I am struck by how Cathy and Dave are both so invested in all their children and their lives together, while still maintaining an incredibly strong relationship with each other. When they go out, they go out together. They talk about everything — not just their children but also happenings in the world as they relate to cultural trends. By helping others in their community, they show their children the importance of giving to others and how they can make a difference, however small it is. I have been surprised that the time I have spent with them has been pleasantly calm. How can a house with ten children, three dogs, two cats, and two rats be less chaotic than the one I live in with only two children, one dog, and a hamster?

It can only be attributed to the two extraordinary people who have climbed on board to join them on the journey.

Dave: "The kids are incredibly well connected with each other. They know the routines and patterns that we have, so we can all live together in some sense of harmony. Sometimes they really fight and can't stand breathing the same oxygen."

Cathy: "But through all that, they still are invested in each other and have the security of knowing there's someone there that loves them and will help them.

As our conversations come to an end, Cathy comments on their adoption experiences so far: "I think I've come full circle — I used to think adoption was the end-all and be-all, but sometimes it's better for kids to remain in a really good foster home than [in] certain adoptive families, in the long run. We need to find a way for these kids to be connected to some healthy people in their life somehow. Maybe adoption isn't necessarily the answer for some kids. The key is finding them the right connection that will give them the best shot at life."

I ask the next obvious question, which is if they will adopt again. Cathy and Dave will celebrate their fiftieth birthdays and their thirtieth wedding anniversary this year. They are grandparents of two and will soon see their son William be married. It's a big year for the Gilberts, and whatever decisions they make will be the ones that will work for their family.

Cathy: "Part of me knows we have boundaries, and another part says, 'You could do it, you could find a way.'"

Dave has always been fully engaged in their choices in adoption, and he finds it hard to think that their lives may not have room for another child. One day their sixteen-year-old son Alex had a friend over to their house who then stayed for dinner. The boy was living with his older brother without their parents and was having some challenges in his life. He commented on what a great dinner Cathy had made and expressed his appreciation of her efforts. He said he wasn't used to having such delicious food. Cathy and Dave were both troubled by his situation and wondered to themselves what would become of him. Later that evening, Dave told Cathy that he needed to make a doctor's appointment for the next morning. "Why? What's wrong?" she asked. Dave calmly replied, "I think I should have my heart removed."

Photo by Rebecca Craigie.

The Gilberts' extended family, including their first grandchild, and another arriving soon.

It remains to be seen if the Gilberts will have room in their lives for another child, but they will most certainly have room in their hearts.

Photo by Angela Colwell.

Let me tell you the secret that has led me to my goal.
My strength lies solely in my tenacity.

Louis Pasteur

Our Red Thread
The Croteau Family
Castlegar, British Columbia

"An invisible red thread connects those destined to meet, regardless of time, place, or circumstance. The thread may stretch or tangle, but never break."
— Ancient Chinese proverb

AT FIRST, THE prospect of flying in a Dash 8 over the Rocky Mountains was at best ominous. But as I head to the storybook town of Castlegar in British Columbia's central Kootenay region, the breathtaking landscape turns my angst into awe. After safely landing, I step out of the plane and feel the blast of frigid air on my face. It is a refreshing contrast to the mild rainy air of Nanaimo. I knew I would enjoy this adventure. When I go to pick up my rental car, I learn the proprietor of the Mountain Retreat Bed and Breakfast, where I will stay tonight, called ahead to make sure I'm given a car with snow tires. Snow tires? Of course … the name of the bed and breakfast is apropos: it is, in fact, on a mountain, with a road leading to it that resembles a paperclip on an incline. If it weren't for the snow tires I would surely end up in the Columbia River.

I have been looking forward to meeting Carrie Croteau, who contacted me in the early stages of researching this book. Carrie is a single mother of three biological children: Jordan, age seventeen, Jarred, age fifteen, and Carlee, age fourteen. She is also adoptive mom to Meigan, age six, and foster mom to three children under five. Yes, that adds up to seven — for now. This was explanation enough for the countless times over the last few years that connecting with her could take weeks. There was simply no time to fit me in!

Carrie loves every part of caring for children and has always had the desire to adopt and foster as many children as possible. During her marriage this vision could not be realized, but after separating from her husband in 2000, she began to turn her dreams into reality.

Carrie remembers sitting on a beach with her mother, telling her about her plans to adopt. There was some concern on her mother's part about the idea, because of Carrie's marital status. This skepticism came from other sources as well, but Carrie remained undaunted. After researching her options, Carrie focused her attention on China.

"I always felt a deep empathy for the abandonment of baby girls in China, and I knew that my daughter was there. I just knew," she says.

Carrie also knew that one of the keys to success would be to work with an agency that believed in her, and she found it in Children's Bridge, an Ottawa-based agency that specializes in adoptions from China and other countries. It has gained the reputation of being one of the best, because of the impeccable planning and execution of the adoption process for both the adoptive parents and the children.

"Having three children biologically was easy for me. Adoption, on the other hand, was uncharted territory, a very hard process to go through. You always have to prove yourself, and that you are worthy, even after already parenting three children! The adoption process takes so much patience and commitment, and can be expensive. Calling adoption a 'labour of love' is really the truth. The harder it is, the more rewarding. It is an awesome experience."

After completing the required documentation, including a home study, Carrie's file was completed and sent to China in November 2001. In January 2003, while at work, she received the email she had been waiting for, entitled "Referral."

Carrie: "I was afraid to look at it. I thought, *What if I don't love her immediately?* I called my colleagues in, thinking they could somehow make it all right. All I remember saying was, 'Oh my goodness, she's beautiful,' and my fears evaporated."

Carrie had less than two months to prepare for the trip to China. She decided to take with her her eldest son, Jordan, who was eleven at the time. They went with thirty-five other families as part of Group 137. This group was then divided into three, each going to a different province in China to meet their children.

Jordan proved to be an excellent travelling companion, helping to navigate and partici-pating fully in the adventure. I ask him how much he remembers of the trip. "I remember all of it, especially when we got Meigan. I remember the hotel, and when they took us to the conference room and brought in the babies," he says.

Carrie: "It was surreal. Cindy was our tour guide, and we looked at each other and she said, 'Carrie, I think this is Meigan.' It was Meigan, and she went straight to Jordan and they

Photo by Angela Colwell.

sat on the couch together. Meigan had been in an orphanage briefly and then in foster care with a farm family. Her skin was very dark from spending so much time outdoors and her hair was buzz-cut short. She was beautiful."

When all the paperwork was complete, Carrie and Jordan took Meigan up to their room and replaced all the bundled layers of clothing with an outfit they had brought for her to wear. The following day, March 11, they began their life together with a twelve-day tour of China. Jordan spent the majority of time with Meigan, pushing her stroller, carrying her, and playing with her. She was very comfortable with him from the beginning. Carrie fed, changed, and bathed Meigan, but always wanted Jordan close by.

I ask Carrie if she felt they were being scrutinized by the Chinese as they travelled with Meigan. She answers, "No one official was watching us, but everyone unofficial was. The Chinese were fascinated to see Jordan with Meigan and thought he was beautiful. The people were so very gracious, courteous, and kind. We walked through villages, among the residents. They welcomed us inside their homes, and we felt humbled by how warm they

Meigan and Jordan share a close bond.

were. They kept saying, 'Come again and bring a friend.' They were very grateful to us; in fact, some of the younger men seemed almost embarrassed. I couldn't help wondering what would happen in our country if the tables were turned. Would we be as welcoming?"

Photo by Angela Colwell.

Carrie and Jordan brought Meigan home on a sixteen-hour flight that had thirty-five babies on board — dubbed "the baby flight." They missed their connecting flight from Vancouver but were so anxious to get home that they flew to Penticton, British Columbia, where friends drove them to Grand Forks.

Carrie: "My father jumped in his truck to take us the final stretch, and when we finally got home at 2:00 a.m., Jarred and Carlee got out of bed to excitedly meet their new sister. The following day we all went to a hockey tournament, and Meigan has been in arenas ever since!"

Meigan's transition into the Croteau family has, for the most part, been seamless. She is a cherished member of the community, and there have been no negative comments regarding her adoption.

Carrie: "She shows no self-consciousness about being Chinese — more about being small in stature. There are some Asian families and students in our community, and we do talk about her culture with books and celebrations of Chinese holidays."

Big sister Carlee.

Carlee: "My friends and my brother's friends all love Meigan and play with her when they are around. They have asked interesting questions about her adoption and just want to know about how it happened — there's never anything negative."

Carrie: "I believe Meigan has her own fantasies about China. She is rarely sad, but sometimes when she is, she'll say, 'I miss my mom and dad in China — it's all better there.' I think there's a part of her that's not full."

For Carrie, it seems as though Meigan has been with them always. "When I look at Meigan, I see my daughter, not Chinese — it's just not what I see. Sometimes I will ask my sister (as she makes a face at me) if Meigan still looks Chinese. When I look at a picture of her, I think, *This girl looks Chinese.* But she is Meigan first, then Chinese, and then adopted."

Photo by Angela Colwell.

Carrie, Jarred,
Meigan, Carlee,
and Jordan.

Since Meigan's adoption, Carrie has become a foster parent to three children and hopes to adopt again — this time from Ethiopia. She wanted to provide a Chinese sibling for Meigan, but because of China's new adoption legislation, she can no longer apply as a single parent. She has registered to adopt Ethiopian twins or a young sibling group under the age of three. While she waits for a referral, Carrie has plenty to keep her busy. Many people wonder why and how she does it.

Carrie: "The children I foster are a part of our family — we're all in it together. The children learn to be helpful and good to each other, and that translates into the household. Everyone is used to being in each other's stuff and space. I've concluded that very few people 'get me.' I work, we have hockey four times a week, and I am a Sparks leader. For me, it's normal. People ask, I answer: 'How do you get the laundry done?' It's never done. 'How do you cook for them?' You just cook enough for that many people. 'How do you get them to activities?' You get in the van and drive everywhere."

There's a sense of confidence and self-knowledge about Carrie that is inspiring. She becomes mildly irritated when people question the amount she is willing to take on from an adoption and fostering perspective. "I am the only person who can define my capacity," she says. "I know what I am asking for and what I can give. I have the abilities and the desire to love and parent children for as long as they are dependant. I do, however, think that all kids deserve to be with their biological parents if they can be taken care of in ways they deserve."

Carrie works as a nurse in the field of adult mental health and has a keen interest in Down Syndrome children. She has a strong desire to adopt an infant with the disorder because she is a believer in and advocate for early intervention with these children, to increase their chances of more positive outcomes.

In the short time that I have been in her presence, I have become convinced that Carrie can accomplish any goal she sets for herself. Even the beautiful mountains in Castlegar are not too high for her to climb. As long as the root of her goals is the love for a child, anything is possible.

Photo by Jill Shantz.

Call it a clan, call it a network, call it a tribe, call it a family.
Whatever you call it, whoever you are, you need one.

Jane Howard

Three Blessings
The Battellino Family
Edmonton, Alberta

"It felt so right … It was like a huge, warm security blanket over all of us."
— Jaime Schroeder, birthmother of Alexis and Austin

THE PROCESS OF adoption is fraught with every emotion felt by human beings. Some are carefully guarded, while others are revealed unabashedly. Susan and Carl Battellino of Edmonton, Alberta, fall into the latter category as they talk about the adoptions of their three children. Before I even met the couple, I expected not only this candid exchange but also the hearty welcome I'm receiving into their cozy family home. Susan declared from our first phone conversation, "I love to talk adoption."

Susan: "We really knew nothing about adoption and had directed so much time and energy into dealing with infertility issues that we didn't consider it. A nurse from the clinic spoke to us about the idea of adoption, and we decided to get some information, not imagining where this path would lead us. We attended a workshop facilitated by a private agency in Edmonton on open adoption. We met couples just like ourselves who were going through the same struggles. Then it didn't seem so odd, and in talking more and more with others, open adoption became more 'normal' for our hope of having a family. I thought, *We really want a baby — and why should the person who has given birth to the baby lose contact?* I think I would feel too guilty about that happening."

Susan and Carl decided to concentrate on adoption to form their family, and they registered with the agency. More than two and a half years later they were still waiting, and they wondered why they were not being matched with a birthmother.

Carl: "We had several friends who were being selected, and that made us feel like there was something wrong with us. Did we need a different house, or two rabbits and a few horses? We are simple, everyday people, not professionals — it was so frustrating."

Susan and Carl were reassured by their adoption worker, Sheila Feehan, that when the right match happened, they would know it. They were about to experience this first-hand, with a young woman named Jaime.

Jaime Schroeder has a close girlfriend who is an adoptee. Jaime talked to her friend about her feelings frequently as she searched for her birthmother, who unfortunately passed away before they could meet. When Jaime discovered she was pregnant, those insights were helpful in her journey to decide what would be best for her baby. She gave birth to a beautiful baby girl, Alexis Jade, on July 19, 1997.

Jaime: "I didn't know what to do; I had not looked for resources and knew nothing about where to start. A nurse in the hospital gave me some pamphlets that started me thinking about the possibility of open adoption. I called an agency, and one of their social workers came right away. It was Sheila Feehan. She was so reassuring in her explanation of the whole process, but it was very overwhelming. My father, best friend, and brother were there to offer support, no matter what my decision. I was given six or seven photo albums to look at of hopeful parents. It was such a huge decision to make for a life — my baby's life. I kept going back to Susan and Carl's profile, because there was just something about it, and they also wanted openness. It felt right. I chose them to be parents to Alexis without even meeting them."

Susan: "When we found out we had been matched, we could hardly contain our excitement and emotions. We had less than twenty-four hours to prepare. I picked Carl up at his office, and we just stood and hugged and cried and cried. All his co-workers, who knew how long we had waited, joined in, and before long we were all a soggy mess. We had set the nursery up already in anticipation of this moment."

Carl: "I remember being awake at 3:00 a.m., we were cleaning the house and thinking, *We're having a baby tomorrow*. We couldn't talk because we would cry. It was overwhelming. What if she changed her mind?"

Jaime: "I was in the hospital for three days with Alexis, but decided not to have much contact with my baby girl. I guess I was afraid of bonding with her and then second-guessing my decision. The hardest time for me was the day I left the hospital without her."

Susan: "When we arrived at the hospital to bring Alexis home, it was the first time we had met Jaime. We only spent a few minutes together, but I felt our connection was instant. While we felt so blessed and ecstatic to become parents of this precious baby girl, we felt such sincere empathy for Jaime. It broke our hearts trying to imagine how she must have felt."

Jaime: "I had two friends with me when I left, and at that moment I was okay with it, because I knew I would see her again. The support I had from Sheila Feehan was so very important, and in the first week afterwards I had my family and friends all around me. I was at peace with my decision."

Susan: "Like all new parents, our initial adjustment to having a new baby to care for was nerve-wracking, but she was such an easy baby and soon everything fell into place."

Two weeks later Carl and Susan welcomed Jaime into their home for the first visit with Alexis together.

Jaime: "We were all so emotional. I found it so exciting to see how great she was doing; to see her house, room, backyard. It was very comforting to know she was in a good place, where she should be. It felt so right, and just as it was supposed to be. If I hadn't felt like that, I would have been worried. It was like a huge, warm security blanket over all of us."

When Alexis was four years old, Susan and Carl were chosen by another birthmother considering adoption for her baby. The experience that followed was a stark contrast to their adoption of Alexis. On November 14, 2001, a baby girl was born by C-section to a twenty-nine-year-old woman considering adoption for her baby. The baby's birthgrandmother was interested in openness because she was raising a half-sister of the baby and wanted the two girls to know each other. While her baby was still in the hospital the Battellinos went to meet the birthmother at her home.

Susan: "Carl and I were so nervous, we didn't know what to expect as we sat at the kitchen table in the birthmother's apartment. After about forty minutes of us describing our family's life, she stood up and said, 'That's all I need to know.' Carl and I looked at each other, realizing that was our cue to leave! It was such a different experience than Alexis's adoption. With Jaime we felt connected immediately, and here the atmosphere was decidedly impersonal. By the end of the day, Sheila Feehan called to say that we would become the parents of another daughter. The following day en route to the hospital we decided Amy would have the middle name of Rose. She had been there for eight days, waiting for some-

Photo by Jill Shantz.

one to hold her and love her, and we were so anxious to bring her home and do just that. In less than an hour at the hospital we joyfully welcomed nine-pound, two-ounce Amy Rose into our family. Before we took Amy home, we stopped to share Alexis's new baby sister with Jaime. She was so happy for us."

Unfortunately, neither Amy's birthmother nor her birthgrandmother has chosen to have contact with the Battellinos. From their perspective, their door will always be open, and they are hopeful for Amy's sake that her birth family will one day change their minds. Amy does ask, "How come we don't see her, like with Jaime?" Susan answers,

Carl, Susan, Austin, Amy, Alexis, and Jaime.

"Sometimes adults have a hard time dealing with painful things, so instead they decide not to talk about them." Susan has some photographs of Amy and a teddy bear to give to her birthmother if the day ever comes that she feels ready to meet her.

During the years before Amy's arrival, Carl and Susan enjoyed regular contact with Jaime, along with get-togethers for birthdays, holidays, and other times Jaime's schedule allowed. There was no set schedule because she is regarded as family and welcome anytime. It was not a surprise that when Jaime became pregnant again, Susan was the third person she called.

Susan: "We cried on the phone together, and I told her if she needed anything to let us know."

Jaime: "I was twenty-five, and it was more difficult to decide what I was going to do. I didn't want to give Susan and Carl the impression that I was going to place the baby with them until I made a decision, although of course they would have been my first choice."

For two weeks Jaime weighed her options, and in mid-January of 2003, seven months into her pregnancy, she once again called Sheila Feehan to begin the adoption of her baby by the Battellinos.

Susan: "Jaime's decision to place her second baby with us brought out a wide range of emotions. We were stunned and humbled. We were worried that she had felt an obligation to choose us because of our special relationship we had already established. It was so much harder now because we now loved her and considered her a family member. We had not thought about the possibility of having a third child and were very concerned about one-year-old Amy feeling left out. Alexis and the new baby would be biologically connected. Jaime completely understood our concerns and respected our need to really think our answer through."

The Battellinos said yes, and on March 23, 2003, Austin Robert was born in the same hospital as his sister, Alexis.

Susan: "We missed his delivery by fifteen minutes, but arrived with Alexis and Amy to be with Jaime and the baby. It was a familiar setting, and even the nurses were the same! For three days I could see the hurt in Jaime; I thought, *Is she sure she wants to do this?* We were so emotionally attached to each other that it was harder for all of us. When it was time to bring Austin home we drove Jaime home from the hospital. I went into the house with her where she gave me gifts for Austin from her family and friends. I left her alone in her house, my heart aching for her but full of love for our new baby boy."

As I hear this group recount their experiences, the love, respect, and gratitude for one another is palpable. There are many tears shed as we talk, but it is obvious that there are no regrets. They share a deep love for these children and are committed to giving them the life they deserve. As they have openly shared their stories with others, there have been mixed reactions. Extended family on all sides and close friends are more than supportive. With others it can be different. Jaime carries pictures of the children with her always and speaks about their adoptions with no hesitation. She says, "Most people are shocked and say thinks like 'How did you do *that*?' and 'So they're not really your kids then.' Some people just can't understand and therefore show silent acceptance."

Photo by Jill Shantz.

Susan, Austin, Alexis, and Jaime.

Susan: "We attended a weekend workshop once and shared our experiences. During this and at other times, it has become evident that many people know little about adoption, and especially open adoption. Many people don't want to make the effort to learn. Once, a couple at the workshop were particularly abrupt in their questioning. You could tell they were very uncomfortable with openness, and they felt there should be established guidelines to be followed. It was disappointing to see this attitude."

While Jaime, Carl, and Susan take any opportunity to enlighten others regarding open adoption, they continue to cherish their own relationships. Alexis, who is now eleven, is very open about her adoption and took great pride in bringing Jaime to school for "bring a relative to school day." Another time when they visited Jaime at her work, a little girl asked Alexis who her mother was. Alexis answered, "That's my mom and that's my birthmom."

This family looks forward to sharing life together going forward. There will be weddings, birthdays, and graduations. There will be laughter and tears. And there will certainly be talking — lots and lots of talking!

Susan: "Jaime gave birth to two of our children. She is truly their family. We were just lucky enough to be chosen to be their parents. Jaime has the gift that they require: the gift of her love and her honesty. It is so important for the children. They will never have to wonder if their birthmother loved them."

Photo by Shelley Weber.

A baby is a blank cheque made payable to the human race.

Barbara Christine Seifert

Miracle Off Ice
Hayley Wickenheiser
Calgary, Alberta

"Every kid needs to know where they came from."
— Hayley Wickenheiser

IT IS A perfect autumn day, and the campus of the University of Calgary is blanketed in golden foliage, brilliantly contrasting the clearest of blue skies. I am standing at the hub of the campus, the Olympic Oval. Students are coming and going around me, oblivious to my anticipation at meeting the best female hockey player in the world. Hayley Wickenheiser undoubtedly spends as much time at the Oval as a team member of the X-Treme as she does at home.

Suddenly I see her approach, wearing a warm smile, with hand extended to greet me. I glance around to see if anyone takes notice of Hayley, quickly realizing that her presence here is an everyday occurrence and that for this occasion I am the only one star-struck. Her partner, Tomas, and son, Noah, soon join us, and we settle ourselves in a common area to talk about Noah's adoption.

Hayley and Tomas first met fourteen years ago when she was playing Triple A Midget. Tomas was coaching a team from the Czech Republic and asked a colleague, "Who's that guy at centre winning all the faceoffs?" He was told, "That's not a guy, it's Hayley Wickenheiser." For the next six years, the two would cross paths at various arenas; finally, in 2000, player and coach worked together on the Oval X-Treme. It has been a successful match ever since, due to their shared love and mutual support in hockey and their making family a priority.

Noah was born to Tomas and his former wife prematurely in April 2001, weighing only one pound, ten ounces. Noah smiles a gap-toothed grin and proclaims, "I could fit into the palm of my daddy's hand!" Today he is a healthy, active seven-year-old who clearly enjoys being in this threesome. He listens intently as his parents tell his story.

After Noah's birth, Tomas was granted sole custody of his son, and he resigned his coaching position to take care of him while Hayley continued in hockey. This created a very close relationship between father and son in the first year of Noah's life, but Tomas was often seen at Hayley's early morning sessions with a bundled Noah in tow. Hayley spent as much

Photo by Shelley Weber.

Noah, Hayley, and Tomas.

Photo by Shelley Weber.

Family fun at
The Oval.

time as she could with him from the moment he was released from hospital at three months, in an effort to bond prior to the process of his adoption.

Hayley: "I never imagined myself becoming a mother at twenty-one, but it was the most natural thing for us to do. Because his birthmother had given consent for me to adopt Noah, I was subject only to background checks of myself and my family: a home study was not required. We began the adoption process when Noah was six months old, and three months later we celebrated its finalization in court. I thought, *This is us — now it's the three of us*."

It has been challenging for Hayley to prioritize family while still pursuing her hockey career. When Noah was two she went to Finland without Tomas and Noah.

Hayley: "It was very hard on everyone. I only saw Noah once every four months. It is very important to me that he is happy and comfortable, thus the decisions I make now are determined by what is best for our family first, hockey second."

Noah knows about and understands his adoption. He spends time with an older stepsister and is close to her, happy to remain connected to his birth family and to look like his sister. I ask the couple about the possibility of expanding their family before Tomas and Noah head out to a swimming lesson.

Hayley: "I would consider adopting again. I don't feel less of a parent because I did not give birth to Noah. I was with him from three months onward. I have always been involved with children's charities, such as Right to Play and KidSport, and believe that our youth are our most important resource. Canada is a melting pot of so many cultures and family types, and it is commonplace to see families of mixed heritages. In the case of adoption, every kid needs to know where they came from, no matter how uncomfortable it may be for us. The important message is that they know we love you and are here for you. I believe more families should consider adoption, especially of the children here in Canada that need families. Having a permanent and loving home has such an important and positive influence on who they become."

All Canadians who follow women's hockey vividly remember the image of Hayley hoisting Noah on her hip around the ice following her team's winning Olympic gold in Salt Lake City in 2002. Hayley Wickenheiser has shown our country that she is still at the top of her game, having been named C.P. Female Athlete of the Year for 2007.

As we end our time together and walk into the brilliant sunshine, Hayley rushes to meet her son at his swimming lesson. It has become evident to me that she is a winner at something much greater — being mom to Noah.

Photo by George Fraser.

The bond that links your true family is not one of blood,
but of respect and joy in each other's life.
Richard Bach

Prairie Dreams
The Mapstone Family
Pierceland, Saskatchewan

"I had nasty phone calls from friends and their mothers who would say, 'You might as well throw her in a trash can …'"
— Terri Lynn Cloutier, birthmother of Mya

WHY IS IT, I wonder, that I can easily navigate suburban Ontario but miss the road three times to a farmhouse in rural Saskatchewan — Pierceland, to be precise. Feeling like a helpless city slicker, I resort to my cellphone to call Juanita Mapstone to rescue me. Pierceland is located just over the Saskatchewan border, twenty minutes east of Cold Lake, Alberta. The three-and-a-half-hour drive from Edmonton has embodied the stark beauty of the Prairies in seemingly endless fields of hay and cattle — lots of cattle.

Once settled in the Mapstone kitchen, it is good to see welcoming faces other than those of … well … cattle.

Juanita and her former husband, Aaron, were quite experienced in the maze that is adoption when the fourth possible opportunity to adopt their second child presented itself. Their initial journey had begun from their home in Medicine Hat in 1997 with applications and home study approval, and the expectation of a long wait. As a result of networking, however, they were matched the following December with a baby boy. Mason Jesse was born five weeks prematurely on January 13, 1999, and his adoption was facilitated by a private adoption agency in Alberta.

Juanita: "What a roller coaster of emotions flooded over us as we stared at our new baby boy in the NICU. We were overflowing with both joy about Mason and sadness for the loss this young couple was feeling."

Juanita maintained a relationship with Mason's birthmother, Kelly, and on one of her visits she learned Mason would be having a sibling. Juanita was again asked to parent the baby, but it was not to be. The birthmother fled to Quebec and eventually lost custody of the little boy, who is Mason's full brother. It was heart-wrenching for the Mapstones. Tyler is now eight and is living with a great-aunt who sends photos once a year to Kelly. Because Juanita has maintained contact with Kelly, Mason is able to see the pictures of Tyler. In 2007, Mason had the opportunity to meet his birthparents and three other siblings during a family vacation.

Juanita: "He was quite overwhelmed, I think, but I will continue to keep in touch with his birth family. I feel it is very important."

After two more failed placements, now becoming frustrated with government red tape, the couple registered with a different adoption agency. Before they had a chance to update their home study, they were contacted on May 20, 2003, with the news of a potential match with a baby girl. And here is where the story begins again.

Terri Lynn Cloutier was seventeen and her boyfriend, Eric Carrier, was twenty when they found themselves facing parenthood. Eric himself is an adoptee, but neither he nor Terri Lynn knew anything about the process. With her mother Brenda's support, Terri Lynn attended a Pregnant Teens program in their hometown of Grande Prairie, Alberta, hoping to find some direction.

Brenda: "The program was geared to helping teens decide between abortion or parenting. The topic of adoption as an alternative was not part of it. I don't remember how adoption became a real consideration. I think we picked up a pamphlet somewhere and, by chance, called the agency where Juanita had registered. I was prepared to support Terri Lynn in whatever decision she made."

Eric: "I and my family also supported any decision Terri Lynn felt was best for our baby, as difficult as it was."

The young couple relied on close family to help them through the ordeal.

Brenda: "We met with two families that were very negative experiences, and we wondered if this meant we shouldn't be considering adoption. Because Mya was born a month prematurely, it was all the more stressful. The two weeks in hospital was spent looking over fifteen profiles. The one that stood out was Juanita's. There was so much in it about Mason and their family, not about what material possessions they had. She showed a lot of concern and empathy for Terri Lynn, and we felt sure that they were the right family for Mya.

Photo by George Fraser.

Mason, Juanita, Terri-Lynn, Brenda, Eric, and Mya.

"We spent the two weeks at our home with Mya just loving her. We closed the door and shut out the world. We had Juanita's profile with us, and we knew what was going to happen."

With only forty-eight hours' notice, Juanita, Aaron, and Mason travelled the eleven hours to Grande Prairie from their home in Medicine Hat. "We spent the good part of a day with Terri Lynn and Brenda, our family falling in love with tiny and adorable Mya Jayde."

As wonderful as their day together was, it unfortunately became overshadowed by the mishandled placement the following day. Even now, it is still a painful example of how the system can sometimes fail families during their most emotional and fragile moments.

Juanita: "The agency and social worker insisted that we meet at a neutral location, and they decided the local A&W would be appropriate. Can you imagine … all these people at an A&W being witness to something as emotional and significant as this? It was just terrible. The social worker was cold and pushy during the process. Despite all of this, I promised Terri Lynn and Brenda that Mya and our family would always be a part of our lives. What I said that day was my word."

Brenda: "We asked Juanita if we could come to see them in a week, which we did. It was great. Juanita had Terri Lynn help her set up Mya's bedroom."

Terri Lynn: "It felt so warm and comfortable spending time with them. I remember falling asleep on the couch with Mya."

And so it went every two months for the next eight months: Brenda, Terri Lynn, and other family members travelled twenty-two hours back and forth to spend time with Mya.

Brenda: "The long, tiring drives didn't matter — it just did not matter."

These visits began a commitment and resolve that would help to see them through the relentless criticisms they would suffer back at home in Grande Prairie. There were many people who could not accept their decision to place Mya and who very harshly expressed their opposition.

Brenda: "In the beginning, the reactions were the same both verbally and with only facial expressions: they said, 'How could you give your child away?' They were so judgmental, but I could understand it, because without the experience and education I could never have accepted it either."

For Terri Lynn, who felt the brunt of the criticism, the memories still evoke tears of pain. "My mom and sister were the only ones that stood by me. I had nasty phone calls from friends and their mothers who would say, 'You might as well throw her in a trash can; otherwise what are you?'"

Brenda: "For the first month after Mya was placed, I stayed by Terri Lynn's side. I routinely

Photo by George Fraser.

(from left) Eric, Brenda, Terri Lynn, Mya, Mason, Juanita, and Harvey.

played baseball, and one night when they knew I was gone they took the opportunity to harass her, and halfway through the game she called me in tears. It was sickening."

Grande Prairie seems to be a town that was slow to change. But perhaps it might take one person at a time.

Terri Lynn: "The person that treated me the worst of all has since apologized to me. She now knows how I must have felt because she has had two children and is a single mom. It took two and half years, but she realizes that my decision was the best one for me and Mya. Things between us have improved."

Brenda and Terri Lynn made an attempt to educate more people by speaking about their experience at the Pregnant Teen program. They spoke about the importance that openness played in the most difficult decision of Terri Lynn's young life. Unfortunately, they were never invited back.

I ask Juanita if Mason asks questions about the open relationship with Mya's birth family.

Juanita: "To Mason, they are just family. He is treated just as Mya — part of their family, and to Brenda he is her grandson. One day Mason asked me, 'Did you come out of your mommy's tummy?' to which I said, 'Yes.' Mason replied in a matter-of-fact tone, 'I didn't — I have a tummy mommy!'"

The families, including Mya's birthfather, Eric, keep in touch regularly by email and phone. Juanita sends photos of all occasions that Terri Lynn and Brenda can't share with them. "You hope the people at the other end feels like they are a part of it," she says. Juanita's partner, Harvey, plays an active role in helping her parent Mya and Mason, and joins their extended-family gatherings when possible. At least twice a year they plan camping trips and weekends at West Edmonton Mall.

Juanita: "Some people still do not understand how we can have such an open relationship, but I think it is wonderful for Mya and for her birth family. I love them dearly."

It is evident to me that love is the glue keeping these relationships strong. It has come from cherishing two children, for whom everyone wanted the best.

Photo by Tobias Beharrell.

Siblings are the people we practise on, the people who teach us about fairness and kindness and caring, quite often the hard way.
Pamela Dugdale

Best Laid Plans

The Grabowski Family
Hamiota, Manitoba

"We thought, *We have a baby coming home, we have to get stuff!*
I opened up the Sears catalogue and ordered everything."
— Adam Grabowski

IN EVERY ADOPTION, there occurs one predictable element: the process is entirely unpredictable.

This proved to be the case for Adam and Marina Grabowski. I have driven three and a half hours northwest of Winnipeg to the small town of Hamiota to hear the story of the family they wondered if they would ever have.

The couple married in 1988, both just past twenty, thinking that they had plenty of time to plan for children. Marina was the architect of their plan, which unfortunately had not come together four and half years later. Determined to be a mom, she began to research adoption. Children and Family Services (CFS) in Manitoba told them that it could be a ten-year wait for an infant. In discussion with adoption workers with CFS, they were given advice to improve their chances.

Adam: "They told us to tell everyone about our hopes to adopt, because connections can be made this way. The week after the course, I was at a meeting and mentioned our adoption plans to a colleague. I was shocked when he said he had a friend who knew of a baby boy needing an adoptive home."

The boy was Native — Ojibwa/American Sioux — and his birthmother was living off the reserve. She had been in foster care as a child herself and did not want her son in the foster care system. Independently, she placed her son in the foster home in which she had lived and looked for a family to adopt him.

Adam: "We met with the birthmom and foster family, learned that the birthmom was hoping for some openness. Before we completed the adoption course I did not 'get' openness, but now I realize the benefits."

What could have been a very long wait instead became an urgent need to complete their home study and necessary paperwork. Less than a month after Adam had had that casual conversation, the couple had the opportunity to bring three-month-old Jordan home.

Adam: "I am a teacher and had shared our adoption news with my students. I asked them to keep it to themselves until everything was finalized. Jordan's homecoming was so unexpected we thought, *We have a baby coming home, we have to get stuff!* I opened up the Sears catalogue and ordered everything. The delivery truck showed up at the school, and thankfully the driver came to the back door of the school. He approached the first classroom, which is mine, and asked, 'Is there an Adam Grabowski here? I got a lot of baby furniture here!' The whole class took part in the operation, with the girls watching the hallway and the boys helping unload. We hid everything in the corner of the room until I came back at midnight to bring it all home. While Jordan was with Marina at her parents' home, I got everything ready for his arrival."

Photo by Tobias Beharrell.

Adam and Jordan.

Photo by Tobias Beharrell.

Vincent, Adam, Jordan, Marina, Adam, and Mikaela.

Jordan's placement with Caucasian parents would not happen today, because of his Native status. Adam and Marina have embraced his culture by attending powwows, workshops with non-Native families who have adopted Native children, meetings with elders, and a weekend camp that included time in a sweat lodge. These efforts to keep his heritage alive are essential components of his development.

When Jordan was two and a half, an agency with the family's file informed them about a potential opportunity to adopt a baby that was located in northern Manitoba, nine hours north of Hamiota. After having made the long trek with Jordan and spending time with the mother and her baby, they left with nothing but mixed emotions. The birthmother had made the decision to parent her baby.

As difficult as their experience was, a month later fate once again stepped in. Child and Family Services in Brandon called one Wednesday to tell them that a baby boy of Native descent had been born six days before. They asked, "Would you like to take him home on Friday?"

Adam: "I think we were chosen partly because the workers knew we were okay with openness, and the birthmother wanted to meet us. The baby, who was Métis/Ukranian, was born in Portage La Prairie just as Jordan and Marina were."

Marina: "Adam was a challenge because he was the baby of the hospital staff in Portage. For the first ten days of his life, he was held constantly and taken around to meet the people staying in the hospital. It took us a while to get him used to a different routine."

I ask Adam and Marina about the differences in their boys' adoptions.

Adam: "The idea of openness was not even considered at CFS in Portage. The Brandon office was the first branch to look at the option. Even though we initially met Adam's birthmom, his adoption remains closed. He has a desire to meet and see his birth family, particularly his birthmother."

Young Adam is aware that his birthmother faced many difficulties that kept her from parenting him but understands how lucky he has been. One day, on the way home from one of his hockey games, he said to his dad, "I guess if I was with my birthmom, I might not be playing hockey." Adam and Marina will support him if he chooses to search for her when he turns eighteen. In contrast, Jordan sees his birth family usually twice a year, sometimes taking young Adam with him. This is a time that can be a bittersweet for him.

When Adam turned one, Marina began working on plans for the adoption of a third child, but in the midst began feeling exhausted and unwell and gaining weight. "I chalked it up to being a very busy mom. I had been told that I would never conceive a child, but did a home pregnancy test just in case. I was shocked when a plus sign showed up! Our third son, Vincent, was born in March of 1997, and Mikaela followed in 2002."

Mikaela was born with Down syndrome. As we talk she is joyfully playing with toys and singing. I believe she is exactly what this house of active boys needs. Physically the children are very different: Mikaela red-haired as her great-grandmother, Vincent blond, Adam brunette, and Jordan black-haired.

Marina: "One day while we were visiting friends, they commented on how red Mikaela's hair was getting. One of their older children asked how she had red hair because Adam and I

Photo by Tobias Beharrell.

do not. Before we could explain the family connection, their six-year-old daughter piped up and said, 'It's the only colour left!' I felt that it showed how accepting and understanding kids can be about any differences. To her, it did not matter that our family has different hair or skin colour in it."

Adam: "We are a poster family for multiculturalism. We have never felt any criticism or judgment in having our boys, and the Native community has been warm and welcoming. The experience of parenting Native children has opened a whole new world to us. We have become more aware of racial profiling. We talk openly with the boys about how others may perceive them. They feel pressure to be extra careful, because they will be watched more. And we agree with them when they say that's not fair."

Marina: "Sometimes I feel as though I have four kids with special needs. Jordan has had some learning struggles but is a natural athlete. I have had to advocate for Adam, because he marches to his own drummer. Vincent feels frustrated in being the youngest brother, but does well in school and sports. It's sometimes easy to leave him out of the loop because he manages quite capably."

Marina shares this perspective on having both adopted and biological children: "When Vincent was born, some people in our community saw him as our first real child. A woman said to me, 'It must feel good to be a real mom and have a child of your own,' to which I replied, 'They're all my real kids. They were only imagined before the day each one came into my life.'"

The drive back to Winnipeg provides me with time to contemplate the diverse yet harmonious portrait of the Grabowski family of Hamiota, Manitoba. I conclude that Marina's plan for this family really did come to be.

Photo by Liz Lott.

A birthmother puts the needs of her child above the wants of her heart.

Sky Hardwick, founder of Life Mothers

Jacob's Lesson
The Franz Family
North Bay, Ontario

"He needed them and they needed him,
and their finding each other seemed to be destined."
— anonymous

MARLEE AND RANDY Franz are a very special couple. At the beginning of my dream of creating this book, Marlee was the first person to contact me to express interest in participating. She sent me an email on November 30, 2003, and in the years since I have had the privilege of sharing in their adoption journeys. Much has happened since then, and the Franz family has played a part in my journey as well.

I felt very encouraged when I heard from Marlee, for several reasons. She and her family live in North Bay, Ontario, and I have been visiting my sister and her family there for ten years. I could sense from Marlee's emails, and later from our phone conversations, that she and Randy were salt of the earth. This is confirmed the first time they welcome me into their comfortable home on a stunning treed lot overlooking Trout Lake. If I were a kid, I'd want them to adopt me.

Marlee and Randy have a wonderful marriage and wanted a family to share their joy in life. As with many other couples, they struggled with infertility while looking into adoption. They were just finishing their home study in May 2002 when a personal connection with a local physician made them aware of a young pregnant woman who was considering adoption. (There were several people in the chain of communication, including a special friend whom Marlee describes as "earning her angel wings" for being instrumental in bringing their first child to the couple.) Less than three days later, Randy and Marlee sat in a room with Lisa Lee, a young woman who would make a courageous decision that would change all of their lives forever.

Lisa: "I was twenty when I became pregnant and was on the threshold of going to college. I really knew that I wasn't in a position to raise a child, and I talked to my friends and family about what to do. One friend in particular who is a lawyer helped a great deal in supporting me and said she would help me if adoption was something I wanted to think about. I considered three couples, none of whom seemed to be the right fit. Then I learned through a friend of a friend that there was a doctor in North Bay who could possibly help."

Marlee: "Randy and I were so nervous meeting Lisa for the first time. Lisa's friend, who happens to be a lawyer, and her social worker colleague were there to help facilitate our conversation. We talked for over an hour about many things, including our similar heritage, our thoughts on names, and [our] expectations after the baby was born — and even if I would take the baby to swim classes! It was very helpful to have two facilitators there to help guide us."

Lisa: "As soon as I saw Marlee and Randy it felt right. I knew in the first ten minutes that I wanted them to adopt my baby."

Marlee: "We sat outside of the meeting room for a little while, and Lisa's lawyer came out to tell us that she was very impressed with us and wanted to proceed with placing her baby with us! We left the meeting thinking, *What just happened?* Everything was moving so quickly; it all seemed too good to be true! On the way home in the car I called our social worker to tell him the news, and we spent the weekend trying to rein in all of our emotions. We were going to have a baby!

"Lisa invited us to go with her to three doctor's appointments before Jacob was born. I think it was awkward and strange for us all, but exciting at the same time. On the first visit we heard the baby's heartbeat, and I tried to imagine who belonged to that heartbeat. Lisa also gave us a card to congratulate us on becoming parents. She wrote that although she had only met us once, she knew we were the best possible choice as parents for her child. On the outside Lisa was maintaining a brave front, but on the inside I think it was a different matter. I also tried to put myself in Lisa's shoes … but I couldn't. I thought, *What a courageous young woman*. At the next visit, Randy and I gave Lisa a card expressing our feelings about the experience. We told her how privileged we felt to have met her and the people she felt closest to. We wanted her to know that we felt that by giving her child life, she had made the most loving and generous decision. We felt honoured that she would entrust her child to us, and we had the utmost respect for her strength and courage. We were so thrilled and grateful to share in the doctor's visits and, in doing so, [to] get to know Lisa on a personal level."

The Franzes drove to Bracebridge the night eight-pound, six-ounce Jacob was born on June 4, 2002. They held Jacob twenty minutes after he was born and were overjoyed. It was a dream come true.

Marlee: "When Randy and I arrived at the hospital we saw Lisa labouring in the hall-way. My first instinct was to run to her and hug her because I was just so excited, but I held back. I wasn't sure if this would be appropriate, and thought she might not feel comfortable with us too close. We took our cues from Lisa's two friends [the ones who had been at the initial meeting] and retreated to the waiting room until we were invited into Lisa's room to meet the beautiful baby boy who would be our son."

Lisa and the Franzes had talked about keeping in touch through pictures and letters at three-month intervals in the first year, and once a year after that.

Lisa: "I remember when I got the first package from Marlee. I was at

Photo by Liz Lott.

Randy, Marlee, Jacob, and Lisa.

76

school, and I went into the bathroom to look at it because I could be by myself and it was the quietest place, and I just cried and cried. Even though seeing pictures of him was painful, I wanted these packages; I wanted to see everything and everybody in his life. Marlee always sent more than was required."

I ask Lisa if she ever felt any regret about her decision.

Lisa: "During the three weeks after I signed the initial papers till the adoption would be final, I waffled about my decision. I questioned whether I was doing the right thing for him. My dad was trying to spare me pain, because he said I should have a C-section and not go through the labour and not see, touch, or hold him. He thought it would be easier if I pretended the baby didn't exist. I didn't see it that way.

"When I first got home, all I wanted to do was be alone. I turned on the television for distraction only to tune in to a *Touched by an Angel* episode dealing with adoption. My mother told me to turn it off; she wanted to protect me. I think actually one of the hardest moments was checking out of the hospital after having him. The person at the desk asked me where my baby was. The nursery had not informed the staff about our situation. It was like a knife in my heart. How could they not know?"

The next five years in Jacob's life kept Lisa and the Franzes connected through letters, photographs, and mutual wonderings. The Franzes have kept Lisa in their thoughts and also in Jacob's by sharing pictures and conversation very openly. Marlee and Randy have shed many tears over the years: tears of joy and tears for Jacob's courageous birthmother, Lisa.

Randy: "I can't even imagine what Lisa has been through. Every time I look at Jacob, I see Lisa. It's always emotional for me."

I ask Lisa what it has been like meeting Jacob again after knowing him only through photographs and letters.

Lisa: "I thought about having visits someday — maybe not this soon, but I'm happy that this has happened. My dad didn't think I should come; I guess he still believes it is better to try to forget it. My mom, however, thinks it's great. Sometimes I have thought, *I wish I could have been able to parent him,* and if Randy and Marlee weren't the people they are, it might have been harder. You couldn't ask for two better people. Even with the great job Marlee does in sending me so much in pictures and letters, it's helped so much to see where he is living and see him with his siblings. It's easy to see how happy and loved he is."

Marlee and Randy have two other children: Benjamin, almost four, who was also adopted as an infant, and, to their surprise and delight, a biological baby girl, Hannah, who is now three. Lisa shares her perspectives on the couple having a biological child: "I think it's just great; wonderful! I absolutely loved being pregnant; it's one of the neatest things that could happen to anyone. I'm happy they finally got to experience everything, not only bringing a new baby home but experiencing the whole nine months before."

The experience of seeing Jacob is still quite new, and I ask Lisa if it makes her decision six years ago any easier in her mind.

Lisa: "Oh God, no, never easier. What it does do is make it more real, more set. I'm not going to say it's hard, but I can't say it's easier. It's somewhere in the middle. I don't know if it will ever get easier; that remains to be seen. I do know that Jacob is in a wonderful family, and for that I am very happy. The fact that we have taken this step of seeing one another is a little scary, but I can envision our relationship going on."

For Marlee and Randy's part, having Lisa decide to connect with visits to their home has been wonderful.

Marlee: "The possibility of seeing Lisa came about because of this book. I was hoping she would want to be a part of it and was thrilled that she was willing. Because we have had the experience of an open adoption with regular visits from our second son's birthfather, I felt it could be possible, and now I regret that we didn't initiate it sooner. Maybe we were both waiting for the other to suggest it."

However this new relationship unfolds, it will always be guided by their shared love for Jacob. His adoption has taught them all a lesson that many others in the adoption world have embraced. Things happen for a reason, and although we can experience deep pain on different levels, there can also be joy when we realize who is really at the heart of our decisions.

Marlee and Randy began updating their home study and preparing to apply to adopt again in late 2003 when Jacob was eighteen months old. Only six months later, they were called by their licensee, who told them they had been chosen by birthparents expecting a

Photo by Liz Lott.

Ben and Hannah find willing laps.

baby in late June. Marlee remembers they were winding down from a busy day of celebrating Jacob's second birthday by watching a Stanley Cup playoff game when they got the call. The baby was early, and interestingly had been born on Jacob's birthday. Marlee and Randy travelled to Ottawa meet the birthparents and spend time with the newborn baby boy, and even introduced two-year-old Jacob to him. After the Franzes had spent almost two days with this beautiful baby, the birthparents made the decision not to place him with them. Marlee and Randy were devastated, but again they would learn that there was a reason for this change of heart.

Once again the couple's connection with a local physician allowed for an opportunity to expand their family. One of the other doctors in the practice that had been instrumental in connecting the Franzes with Jacob's birthmother, Lisa, was caring for a sixteen-year-old pregnant teen who was considering adoption for her baby. A meeting was arranged for mid-October, and the Franzes once again sat in a room with a family who could potentially set them on a new course. The baby's birthmother chose not to attend, but her mother did, along with the birthfather, Adam, and his mother, Karan.

Marlee: "I was surprised to see Adam there and not the baby's birthmother. Adam was quiet, shy, and very nervous, but the meeting went very well. We were not going to get our hopes up, though … because of the previous heartache we had experienced."

As I speak with Adam during my second visit with the Franz family, he shares what it felt like to contemplate placing his child with a strange family.

Photo by Liz Lott.

Adam and Ben
share a cuddle.

Adam: "I didn't know anything about adoption, really. I didn't even know that my girlfriend was pregnant until four months into it. She wanted to keep her pregnancy a secret from all of our friends, so I felt I had to cover it up too. I think a lot of that was because of other influences, but it was so difficult for me. Even though my parents encouraged me to begin my first year of university, I decided to delay a year, and work. I wanted to be there for my girlfriend and baby, regardless of her desire to remain emotionally detached."

Marlee: "I was worried about the fact that we had not met the baby's birthmother. I thought it might be a bad sign. We eventually had the opportunity to meet the baby's birthmother at a meeting with everyone present … Adam, both birthgrandmothers, and social workers. Although I was relieved to finally meet the baby's birthmother, it did not allay my concerns about the fate of a little baby's future being in the hand of someone so young."

On December 8, 2004, eight-pound, five-ounce Benjamin was born in the middle of an ice storm. Adam was at the hospital with his mother and the baby's other birthgrandmother. Marlee

80

Photo by Liz Lott.

Fishing fun.

was there too, and stayed with Adam in the waiting room while they both awaited the baby's birth. Marlee was also anxious to have Randy join them, as he flew home from a business trip two provinces away.

Marlee: "When I arrived at the hospital, I wasn't sure what to do or say. I was grateful to be with Adam, as awkward as it felt. I remember Adam's mother asking me how I felt with the birth so imminent: excited, apprehensive … cautious, is how I described it. I was invited to go in and say hello to Ben's birthmom so that she would know I was there. I realized how very young she was, and thought that she must have been so overwhelmed with everything. When I rejoined Adam in the waiting room, I could see he was equally overcome with the experience. My heart went out to him. He said, 'I can't believe what I've put her through,' and I replied, 'But look what you are giving us.'"

Although Ben's birthmother didn't want any formal contact with the Franzes or Ben after his birth, she did come to his room to say goodbye before leaving the hospital. She and Adam also presented the family with a beautiful keepsake for Ben's first Christmas. Marlee and Randy remain hopeful that one day Ben's birthmother will want to meet him. He is an extraordinary little boy. However, they are thrilled that Adam wishes be a part of Ben's life, beginning when Ben was six months old.

Ben is almost four, and as we are talking he climbs on and off Adam's knee in between playing with his trucks and negotiating activities with Jacob and Hannah. I ask Randy how he feels about having his son's birthfather around for visits.

Randy: "I am totally comfortable with it. It's so important for Ben and for Adam."

Adam: "I don't ever want to overshadow Randy as a father figure. Randy and Marlee are Ben's parents, and I feel it is a privilege to have a relationship with Ben and his whole family. He is a part of my life, and I am so happy that he is being cared for surrounded by so much love. I carry a picture of Ben in my wallet and share our story openly. It makes me feel happy to talk about him … not sad. I hope to always be a part of his life."

Randy and Marlee were overjoyed to welcome daughter Hannah in September 2005 and introduce her to her two big brothers. Her arrival was a surprise, as they had been told that biological children were out of the question for them. It is a busy and very happy household, where extended family on both sides come to enjoy special occasions or a day of fishing off the family dock. It is a place where Jacob's lesson continues to teach them all. Things happen for a reason.

Photo by Liz Lott.

Biology is the least of what makes someone a mother.
Oprah Winfrey

Fifty-Three Desperate Days
The Herst/Jackson Family
North Bay, Ontario

"I've always known that I wanted to be a mother, and that it takes
a lot more than nine months and giving birth to be one."
— Alison Herst

THE SHIMMERING WATERS of Lake Nipissing on a perfect July day are a world away
from Haiti. But it is from that country, via the Internet, that a beautiful baby girl captured
the heart of Alison Herst, before they even met.

Alison is experienced in life's tests, the ones that demand extraordinary determination,
strength, and perseverance. So as her story unfolds, you will understand how this single woman survived the ordeal of bringing her daughter home. It started with a childhood dream.

Alison: "I had always been involved in sports as a child, and my brother was in the canoe
club. That led me to start kayaking when I was eleven. I began winning at thirteen, and at
sixteen I won the Canadian championships. The dream was to go to the Olympics, and in
1990 I moved to Ottawa, trained with the Ontario team, and finally made the national team.
It took a lot of physical strength and stamina, as well as mental focus, which paid off when
we went to the Olympics in Barcelona in 1992, where we placed fifth. In 1995 we won
the world championships in Germany. The following summer in Atlanta we lost the bronze
by six one-hundredths of a second. It was very hard, and I made the decision to leave the
Canadian team. By that time, I had met my husband, who was on the Italian team, and after

we married in 1996 I lived in Italy for five years. It was during this time I discovered that accomplishing my next goal might prove more challenging than the Olympics."

Alison returned to Canada alone in 2001, having separated from her husband, still determined to be a parent, even if it meant being a single one. She chose adoption and discovered that her options were somewhat limited going it alone. Alison's parents, Paul and Linda, had always encouraged her to pursue her dreams, and this was no exception. When she decided to focus on a Haitian adoption, their concerns centred on the challenge of Alison being single. Could their daughter do this? No question about it: once Alison made her mind up about something there would be no stopping her.

In the fall of 2002, Alison was immersed in her new teaching career in North Bay. She had connected with the Global Village Adoption Agency near Ottawa and with Precious in His Sight, a Haitian adoption program. On October 30 a friend rushed into her classroom and told her to look on her website. A two-week-old baby had just been listed as available for adoption. It was love at first sight, and that evening Alison wired US$5,000 to put this beautiful baby girl, called Zoe, "on hold." It was the beginning of a year-long odyssey, fraught with obstacles that would test Alison's endurance in a way that would surpass the toughest of kayak races.

Adding to the stress was the shocking and tragic news that her ex-husband had been killed in an automobile accident. It was more than Alison could take, but she would have to put her sadness on hold in order to concentrate on her next goal.

Alison's first trip to Port Au Prince, Haiti, and the orphanage, was in November 2003. Her sister-in-law, who is a physiotherapist, accompanied her so that she could assess Zoe's physical development. In the beginning everything seemed quite organized, with the same driver always picking her up at the airport each of the six times that she went.

Alison: "I remember when we finally arrived, I wasn't surprised at the conditions. The town was very hot, dirty, and busy, and smelled like garbage. Once inside the orphanage, things improved. The first moment I saw Zoe, she was sleeping in her crib, all bundled up. My tears flowed as her nanny, Veronique, scooped her up and put her in my arms. While I held her, Veronique changed her diaper and dressed her up, as they liked to do when we came. I was so elated, and we took her to our hotel, laid her on the bed, and just looked at her."

Zoe appeared to be healthy and robust, but medical testing required by the Canadian government would tell the true state of her health.

Alison and her new daughter spent four wondrous days together, the time allowed on each visit. She felt confident that Zoe was being well taken care of, but worried about her safety. Alison's mother, Linda, recalls her visit to Haiti: "It was like signing a library book out when we took Zoe to the hotel." Alison decided to make a sign with a picture of her that said, "I'm Zoe's mom" to ensure that they knew who her mother was when she was not with her.

Linda: "Zoe was ten months old when I went to Haiti. I fell in love right away. She had an intestinal bug the whole time I was there, but as sick as she was, she was a happy, loving baby. She came into our arms willingly and loved to be held. My biggest fear in all of it was (because we all loved her already) that Zoe's medical tests would uncover something that would prevent Ali from bringing her home, but thankfully she was fine. She is pure joy, and we have so much fun with her. She's our granddaughter."

Alison's father, Paul, travelled to Haiti twice. During the second visit, when it became apparent that their stay would be extended and the orphanage closed, they all moved to Walls Guest House. It was a safe haven that accommodated people from all over the world who travelled to Haiti to help the country in a variety of ways. The challenge was clearly going to be moving the adoption process forward in a country where money is the motivation for progress — which is usually excruciatingly slow.

Paul: "The days turned into weeks as Ali struggled to do everything necessary to get Zoe's dossier and passport in order. At every turn, it was a question of paying someone to get anything done. We were in touch with officials at the Canadian embassy in Haiti every day, who told us their hands were tied until we got Zoe's passport. We settled into an uncertain routine that repeated itself day after day. I would take care of Zoe while Ali made fruitless phone calls. I walked endlessly around the guesthouse courtyard with Zoe and listened to ball games on a portable radio that I had brought. My cholesterol went down to nothing and I lost thirty pounds. I set the alarm on my watch to sound at 4:00 p.m., and our happy hour would begin. Ali and I would sit down, have a beer, and take a break from it all. At night, I would go to bed early, while two armed guards kept watch behind a chained and locked gate. Sometimes we would hear shots as we went to sleep. To this day, I have not reset my watch alarm. Its sound is a bittersweet reminder of one of the happier memories of our time there."

At the twenty-eight-day mark, Paul headed home to recharge for his second visit, and Alison's fiancé was happy to fill the void, even briefly. Stacey Jackson came into Alison's life in the summer of 2002, when she was already on her adoption journey. By the following year, he had fallen in love with this indomitable woman, and, without reservation, he embraced her plan to adopt Zoe. Stacey was in awe of Alison's strength and determination in her fight to bring Zoe home.

His time with them in Haiti only reinforced his desire to be with them forever.

Photo by Liz Lott.

Stacey: "The first time I saw Zoe, I let her control the situation. I am the youngest of twenty-nine grandchildren, and have had a lot of experience with children, but I was new to her world. I was extremely nervous and cautious, but she came to me immediately. It was awesome. We spent the week getting to know Zoe as a couple, enjoying just being together."

Alison: "Stacey was my sounding board and punching bag. He heard very frustration and angry detail of what I was facing. I needed to talk and express my emotions, and when we weren't together, we spoke every day by phone. He was there to listen."

Stacey: "I was able to see first-hand the conditions they were surrounded by: the extreme poverty, no roads, garbage littered, children running everywhere, and putrid smells. When it was time for me to go home, I hated to leave them there. It was so uncertain when I would see them again, and financially it was so difficult. I was relieved Ali's father would be there again."

Alison: "I didn't do very well when I was on my own. Things were still dragging on, I was running out of money, and I felt at

Zoe.

the end of my rope. There was a fine line between being proactive and pissing people off. I cried a lot. I remember one very low moment, when I was crying in frustration and anger, and Zoe climbed up on my lap and put her arms around me. I thought, *This isn't right — I should be taking care of her! I can't believe no one cares — we're doing a good thing!* There was very little support while I was there on my own, but I knew if I got really desperate, I could go to Judy [who ran another orphanage], who lived a few blocks away. I would put Zoe on my back and run — terrified to leave the safety of the walls — over the garbage and past the goats, just for a few hours of support.

"My love for Zoe was what kept me going. I was loud and assertive, and I knew nothing and no one would move unless I made it move. I refused to spend Christmas in Haiti."

Photo by Liz Lott.

Warm embrace from Mom and Dad.

Paul: "When I returned to Haiti, Ali was even more determined to bring Zoe home. It was December, and Zoe was fourteen months old. Within a few days the call we had been waiting for for so long finally came. Pierre, the handler who had been in charge of obtaining Zoe's passport, told us to meet him with US$900 and he would hand it over. It felt like a cloak and dagger operation."

Alison: "Our driver took us to the specified location, and we parked and waited. Pierre walked towards us and knocked on the window. He said, 'You've been here long enough —now get your daughter out of here.' The money went into his hands as Zoe's passport came into mine. We rushed straight to the embassy, and in only twenty minutes had the visa we needed to leave Haiti for good."

The next day, December 8, 2003, Ali and her father boarded a plane with their precious cargo for the last leg of their incredible journey. Alison called Linda and simply said, "It's over." They both wept with relief and joy.

Alison: "I was numb and so nervous standing in line to get our tickets, because I didn't feel we were out of the clear yet. Someone said to me, 'Take good care of her,' and I looked up to see the welcome sight of an Air Canada sign. I was so exhausted and overwhelmingly relieved. It was surreal. I had been insulated in this foreign world for so long and had no idea of what was going on in the one I'd left behind."

Somewhere in Corpus Christi, Texas, Stacey had stopped at a grocery store on the way home from the gym. Standing in the line, his cellphone rang. The origin of the call was Ottawa, and he remembers wondering who would be calling from there.

Stacey: "I'll never forget it. As soon as I heard Ali's shaking voice I started to cry and almost dumped my groceries. It was incredible. I wanted to drop everything and go to them."

Alison: "The drive to North Bay was excruciating (so close and yet so far). Our story had become well known, and our community had been so supportive, both emotionally and financially during our ordeal. Along with family and friends, the media was waiting when we arrived. Everyone wanted to welcome our beautiful girl home. The emotion of the moment left me almost paralyzed."

Since that happy day, life has settled into the routine of being a family. Zoe's energy and joie de vivre ensures that it is a life far from mundane. She is a happy three-year-old who heartily embraces the adventures of every new day.

Photo by Liz Lott.

Sisters.

89

Alison: "We have been surrounded by love and support as Zoe has made her transition. Some people are a little taken aback when they see us. I don't even see Zoe as black — I see her as my child. In fact, I think she's the spitting image of me with a better tan!

"I still sometimes get irritated when I see people all around me getting pregnant, but I feel honoured and special to be an adoptive mom, to have that quality that opens my heart to love any child. I am also very lucky to have the most incredible fiancé who has stepped into the situation and so willingly shares my dream. We do want more children, and if it happens through adoption, it will be another black child so that Zoe will have a sibling she can relate to.

"Zoe knows she has a 'tummy mommy,' and when she is older we will share everything about her birth history! One day in Haiti her birthmother appeared at my door. She asked, 'Are you Zoe's mom?' I said, 'Yes,' and she said, 'So am I.' She held Zoe as I nervously asked her every question I could think of, in hopes of being able to answer all of Zoe's in the future. I was terrified to lose her — maybe that is the reason I am hesitant about open adoption. My view is that when birthparents cannot take care of their children, adoptive parents need to build relationships with the children who have been entrusted to them. We know that difficult questions will come up for Zoe, and we will always be there to help her as she understands more of her story. If people ask her, 'Where's your real mom?' I'll be there to say, 'I'm right here.'"

Note: Since this writing Alison and Stacey were married on June 24, 2006, and then welcomed baby girl Kiana into the world on November 25 of that year. Zoe is a healthy and active five-year-old. Alison teaches elementary school in North Bay and Stacey is a police officer. Alison's parents, Paul and Linda, are doing well and enjoying being grandparents. The memories of Haiti are diminished by the business of family life but are no less meaningful so long after the day Zoe finally came home. And now she is a big sister and proud of it.

Photo by Kirsten White.

We cannot fashion our children after our desires,
we must have them and love them, as God has given them to us.
Johann Wolfgang Von Goethe

The Chosen Ones
The Shields Family
North Bay, Ontario

"All you have to do is tell your kids you love them every day,
show that you mean it …"
— Steven Shields, son of Jill and Gord Shields

GETTING THE SHIELDS family together in one place for any longer than a few days at a time is no small feat, whether it be in North Bay or Georgetown, Ontario, or in sunny California. I was hoping for California, Steve Shields's current address, but am content to find myself in Georgetown at the home of Christine Ferguson, Steve's sister. Their mother, Jill, has been visiting from North Bay over Christmas. Gord Shields, the family patriarch, passed away in 2004, but I can't help but feel his presence strongly here as his children and wife speak about their family life. The tremendous positive influence he had on all of them as husband, father, and grandfather becomes apparent as our conversation unfolds.

When Jill and Gord realized that having children biologically was improbable, Jill began taking the necessary steps to create a family through adoption. It was 1968, and Jill's health care background taught her that the Children's Aid Society would be the place to start. They undertook the required interviews and approval process, and a year later they were matched with a ten-day-old baby girl. Christine had been in Sick Children's Hospital since her birth, and Jill recalls the day they first met their new daughter.

Jill: "It was July 19, 1970, an excruciatingly hot day in Toronto, and Gordie was dressed in a suit for the occasion (as was typical for him). When we arrived at the CAS office, we knew Christine was there in another room, while we attended to paperwork. We were both so anxious to see her and get out of there. Gord said, 'I don't care what she looks like as long as she doesn't have red hair.' Of course, this was a tongue-in-cheek remark, but wouldn't you know that she had a definite red hue to her hair! What really struck us both was that they gave us the impression that we would have the option, once having met her, that we could say no to adopting her. That totally blew me away. That never even entered my mind! To me, you have what you have, the same as with a biological child."

A year later, Jill began the process for another child, thinking that it would possibly be another two-year wait. This time things moved forward more quickly, and eighteen months later they were matched with a five-month-old baby boy. Enter Steven on December 19, 1972, their Christmas baby. The extended Shields family welcomed him and celebrated brother and sister in a holiday gathering.

Jill: "I remember Gord's mother asking me if we were going to tell everyone about the children's adoptions. We always talked about it as a normal thing. To us it was never an issue. We were so happy and excited to have a family, regardless of how it happened. Once the adoptions were final, they were our family and we treated them as our own. We didn't necessarily bring the topic up, but never tried to hide it."

I ask Steve and Christine if they remember when they learned of their adoptions.

Christine: "I don't remember not knowing I was adopted. My mother would often read an adoption storybook to us called *The Chosen One*. We talked about adoption when I was growing up, but I didn't think about it influencing me in any negative way. Recently, looking back, I do remember that there were times in my life when I did feel very disconnected."

Steve: "Before high school, when kids found out I was adopted they'd think it was cool or say things like 'How much did your parents pay for you?' I grew up with all the advantages a kid could have, but still never felt like I belonged. In college my best friends would joke around or tease me about things and add on the line sometimes 'Just because

Photo by Kirsten White.

Jill, Christine,
and Steve.

your mom found you in a dumpster.' I just laughed it off, but maybe it had more effect on me than I knew. I started to pay more attention to my adoption after my father died."

Steve spent a significant part of his boyhood playing hockey, which ultimately led him to success as a goaltender in the National Hockey League. The connection father and son forged during trips to early morning practices and endless tournaments gave Steve unconditional positive support: his father's phone call to him was his first after every NHL game Steve played. Despite this, Steve still felt an inexplicable disconnect from his family.

Steve: "I just felt different, and as I got older the feelings of insecurity seemed to deepen. The pressure of professional sports was huge. I was afraid of failure. I was afraid of success. And when Dad died, what I was doing didn't seem that important anymore. My mother thinks that because they raised me as if I was their biological son, any emotional issues I face can't necessarily be attributed to being an adoptee. She would say, 'That's just the way you are.'"

Moving around so much has undoubtedly contributed to Steve's feelings of impermanence in his life. He is now able to take more time to explore the uneasiness he feels around his adoption. He talks with his mother more than ever, about everything, which opens the door to greater understanding for both.

In our discussions, we also consider the differences in the timing of Steve and Christine's homecomings. Christine was ten days old when the Shieldses brought her home, but Steven was in foster care for more than five months. Could those early days have contributed to his feelings of impermanence and lack of belonging?

Christine shares her perspectives on her adoption: "I have always expressed my emotions quite openly, and as a teacher have even discussed adoption with my students. When I tell them that I am adopted they usually flip out. Then we talk about deeper questions like, What makes a parent? Is it the couple who conceived me or the mom and dad that took care of me for thirty years? I have friends who are adopted, and I find it interesting that I have gravitated towards other adoptees. Maybe it makes me feel as though I am a part of some community."

I ask Steve and Christine how they feel about knowing more about their birth families or potentially meeting them.

Steve: "I'd like some information about the circumstances of my adoption — about just the mother, though. When I become the person I want to be, then I will think about it. A big part of me asks, 'Why would you give me away?' but then I think it's brave. I don't think I'm angry, just curious."

Christine: "I don't feel a desire or curiosity about meeting my birthmother. I'd be afraid of opening up a can of worms. I have some health background, and I know my birthparents were in their mid to late twenties. I think if I had been in their position at that age, I would have kept the baby. Some adoptees I know have experienced a lot of pain with birth family reunions. I don't know of any positive outcomes."

I am fascinated to hear similar emotions expressed by Steve and Christine regarding one aspect of a potential meeting with their birthmothers. I can sense a fear of the unknown and a reluctance to once again experience a sense of rejection or abandonment, as Steve characterized it. These emotions surface visibly as Christine talks about the birth of her son, Nathan, and how being a mother herself changed her thinking.

"Before Nathan I thought, *How could anyone give up their child?*" she says. "Then, with Nathan's birth, I realized that you will do anything to make that child happy, and if it meant giving him to someone else to make sure he had a better life, then you would do it. If I couldn't have done right by him, I would have done that. I understand it more now. You don't realize how much you will love your child until you have one. I realize that it was not an easy or thoughtless thing for her to do. I don't remember at any point feeling 'left' because I was adopted. It was cemented in my mind that she gave me away because she knew it would be best for me, not because she did not love me."

I observe Jill as she listens to her children to see if any of their remarks surprise or trouble her. She tells me that they have discussed these things before and that she has always been open to ongoing dialogue about their adoptions.

Jill: "When the kids were growing up, they were simply our kids, our family, and they would always be our family. People would often be shocked when we shared with them that Christine and Steve were adopted, because of physical similarities to us. I never drew a separation between adoptive and biological children. We had waited so long to have children, and we expected it to happen; our concern in the adoption process was more will we be good enough, will we be approved and acceptable as parents?"

These questions are perhaps at the root of some of Steve and Christine's observations of their own thoughts and behaviours.

Christine: "I have very few close friends, ones that I want to confide in. I am more concerned about being perceived as competent, good at what I do. Things always seemed to come more easily to Steve, and at times I felt an uphill climb in competing with Steve the NHL personality. I would show my frustrations as a child by stomping off to my room and slamming my door."

Photo by Kirsten White.

Steve: "I think I have spent my life basically distrusting people and never wanting to rely on anyone. My parents certainly didn't do anything to contribute to that. I feel that I did not really connect emotionally with either of my parents, which has translated into other areas of my life. It's almost as though I subconsciously behave in certain ways to test the people I want to love me, to see if they'll leave me if I screw up. I wish that my mother had acknowledged and understood more from the beginning the way I felt and consider[ed] that these feelings could have stemmed from by being adopted. Instead she would say, 'That's just the way you are.' I know I can't use adoption as an explanation for all of my attitudes and behaviour, but I think that is part of it. She'd also say, 'Well, your sister's not like that,' and I wonder now if that's why she was stomping her feet and slamming doors! I am learning to differentiate issues that are adoption-related and those that are not. I know that I am accountable for my behaviour, and being adopted can't justify any of it. A book that I have found very helpful is *Twenty Things Adopted Kids Wish their Adoptive Parents Knew*, by Sherrie Eldridge. I have been able to relate to it a lot."

Christine: "I think I have dealt with my adoption in different ways at various stages in my life. A therapist once told me that some of the personal challenges I was experiencing were probably related to being an adoptee. I now know that the decision my birthmother made took a great deal of courage. Sometimes I wonder if I have [met] or will unknowingly meet someone that I am actually related to. For now that person is my son. These thoughts have still not led me to wanting to find my birthparents. I don't consider them parents in any way at all."

Steve: "Since my father died, my mom and I have become much closer, and we are relating on a new level. I am working on understanding the impact that two major issues have had on me: my feelings of abandonment by my birthmother and the lack of emotional connection with my adoptive mother. I don't think I even told my mother I loved her until we lost Dad. But having said that, I had a great life as a child; my parents were always with us and involved. I can't remember ever not being with my parents at night. I am grateful for them and their adoption of me. If I felt secure in all aspects of my life I would adopt a child myself. The person I feel closest to now is my nephew, Nate, probably because he loves me unconditionally and doesn't judge me. I really think that all you have to do is tell your kids you love them every day, show them you mean it, and stick with them no matter what."

Adopted or biological, this is something all parents should aspire to. The Shields family's story illustrates a very important lesson. We can never fully empathize with feelings that are unfamiliar to us, but we can always acknowledge them — a crucial step towards truly embracing and connecting with those we love.

Photo by Kirsten White.

Somehow destiny comes into play. These children end up with you and you end up with them. It's something quite magical.

Nicole Kidman

Destiny's Child
The Watling Family
Markham, Ontario

"I did not feel like I was losing everything that I had, but more like
I was sharing something that I had already been blessed with."
— Iolo Brown, birthmother to Caroline

THE COOL APRIL rain does nothing to dampen the spirit inside the cozy Markham home. I feel as though I have walked in on an intimate family reunion already underway. Easy laughter fills the air, and at the centre of the gathering is beautiful, brown-eyed Caroline. She is ten years old, and her story is one of joy and openness, not of loss.

In 1994, at age twenty-five, Iolo Brown became pregnant unexpectedly and decided to place the baby for adoption. At twenty-two, she had given birth to a son whom she believed to be a gift to her from God, and she now thought how wonderful it would be to grant this same gift to someone else who could not otherwise have a child.

Coincidentally, Laurie and Bill Watling had been navigating through the maze of adoption procedures for well over a year. Little did they know that their winding path was about to take a defining and life-altering turn, and that they and Iolo were destined to begin a new journey together.

Bill had a co-worker, Pete, who shared with him a dilemma: Pete had been involved in a casual relationship with Iolo, who was now pregnant. He did not know what they were going to do. Bill listened as calmly as he could, although he couldn't believe what he was hearing. He tried to contain his excitement as he explained to Pete his and Laurie's own dilemma involving their desire to adopt.

Two weeks passed. Now in her fifth week of pregnancy, Iolo contacted Bill, and three weeks later, after many long phone conversations with him and with Laurie, a meeting was arranged at Iolo's home. By now, it felt right for all of them. They had connected emotionally and intellectually regarding the future life of the child, and without professional guidance, but with a firm resolve, all anticipated the birth of "their" baby. It was a joyous time, during which they established a deep friendship.

Iolo: "It felt like a surrogate pregnancy from very early on, not like I was giving something up or that they were taking something from me. They were involved in the process every step of the way, and we all learned together. Any negative thoughts I'd had about adoption only related to closed adoptions. One friend in particular had spent much of his late teens trying desperately to find his birthmother. I had also known other birthmothers who had given up their children in closed adoptions, only to wait as long as twenty years to be reunited.

"But I also knew of open adoption, and wanted only that for my baby. That would be the most honest and upfront manner in which to deal with the situation. I wanted to at least have the opportunity to know about this child's development.

"Bill and Laurie and I discussed the concept from the very beginning. I do remember Bill being hesitant about it, worrying that I might want to drop by to visit every Saturday, intruding on their life. Fortunately, and most importantly, we all wanted what was best for the baby while respecting each other's private lives. We were mindful of the level of openness that would work for everyone."

Laurie: "The other quite conscious decision we made was to navigate this course ourselves until such time as we needed to file the legal paperwork. We just felt the fit was so right, and any time the conversation turned to a professional it became more of a negative thing — disheartening.

"It was so thrilling to be able to share in the process, the ultrasounds, and the frequent phone conversations. Iolo was incredibly generous, making sure that I experienced as much of what she was going through as possible. Because I'd had cancer that had ultimately led to a hysterectomy when I was twenty-seven, I did not have to go through the frustration of years of trying to conceive. The reality of never being able to give birth was difficult to accept, but I was alive and healthy and could become a mom another way.

"By the time we took Iolo to the hospital for Caroline's birth, we had already been through so much together. It all felt so natural, so normal to us that we were a bit taken aback by the reactions of the doctor and the nurses, who all seemed so surprised by our arrangement. Bill videotaped the delivery, and when our little girl was born, the doctor asked, 'Who do I give her to?' Iolo replied, 'Why, to her parents, of course.' It was very emotional and joyous."

Bill: "Later, one of the nurses came to the door. [She said,] 'Everyone is talking about you: the whole place is abuzz. Because of you, we are going to re-evaluate our policies on adoption procedures.' We thought that was interesting. The hospital had never seen this amicable an arrangement before, and we were glad that we might help in changing any negative attitudes about adoption."

Photo by Kirsten White.

Bill, Iolo, Caroline, Jonathan, and Laurie.

Laurie: "Initially, when we brought Caroline home I would think about Iolo every single day and wonder how could she have made the decision to give us the most incredible gift in the world. But all along, when we would speak about the baby, I recalled that she would always say, 'Let's talk about what *your* baby did today.'"

Bill: "I look at it a little differently. I feel that Iolo gave Caroline a gift as well: the gift of loving parents and an extended family who would love her too. I have always regarded our relationship with Iolo as one of good friends, not family, and that our friendship exists not solely based on the fact that she is Caroline's birthmother."

Iolo: "When Bill and Laurie took Caroline home, my feeling was that they now had their family and I had mine. I went home to my three-year-old son, Jonathan, and we continued on with our life. He had been aware of the pregnancy, and that the baby in my tummy was going to live with Laurie and Bill. We had occasional visits, but at three years of age, he did not know the details about the adoption.

"When he was about nine years old, we were away with friends who had a six-year-old daughter. Jonathan told me that he wished that he had a sister that age. Laurie and I had always discussed what and how much consistent information to give to the children so that neither would ever feel that the truth had been withheld from them.

"Jonathan was excited to have a sister, and on visits they would play together and act as friends. As parents, we knew that if we always presented the truth, they would never uncover any secrets that might cause divisions in either family relationship."

Photo by Kirsten White.

The laughter
continues …

Laurie: "One thing that has helped over the years is that whenever Iolo got in touch with us, I never felt threatened or that she was checking up to see how 'her' baby was doing. It was always, 'How are you all?' We talk about how both of the children are doing, what is happening in our lives. Anytime Caroline and I talk about her adoption it is matter-of-fact and not anything earth-shattering. She knows that any questions she has will always be answered, by one or by all of us, and as she gets older she will make her own decisions about seeing Iolo and Jonathan."

Iolo: "I feel that the decision I made has had a very positive effect on my life. We are two happy families who are close friends and who keep in touch. In spite of some questions posed to me over the years, I am proud of and totally at peace with the outcome of my choice. It is great to know that I can call at any time and that I am invited to share milestone moments. I think Caroline will be content with her destiny: she has families who love her and will never have to search for her birthmother."

It is hard to imagine an adoption story that has no sense of loss or pain, or any unanswered questions connected to it. But as I speak with Iolo, Bill, and Laurie, and then spend some time with Caroline and Jonathan, the overwhelming impression I have is that they are all content with their journey so far.

From the moment Pete chose to approach Bill, of all his co-workers, fate was put in motion. And, as Laurie stated, "Iolo really was the one who set the tone of the adoption from the beginning." She and the couple she chose to parent her baby were in perfect harmony, and Caroline is destiny's child indeed.

Update: Since the writing of this chapter in 2004, Caroline has become an active and engaging fourteen-year-old. Iolo and Jonathan continue to stay in touch with Caroline, Laurie, and Bill. Our second meeting has the sun shining in Unionville, where Laurie and Caroline now reside. Bill lives in Oshawa and maintains a very close relationship with Caroline. The love and respect they all share is still evident as I watch their comfortable and playful interaction with one another. Life is good — very good.

Photo by Chris Hardy.

A baby is born with a need to be loved and never outgrows it.
Frank A. Clark

Divine Intervention
The Jordan Family
Stouffville, Ontario

"It's like having your own birth child ...
you don't know what's going to come through the door."
— Margaret Jordan, mother of Elizabeth

ON APRIL 7, 1986, a two-pound, six-ounce baby girl was born at Women's College Hospital in Toronto. She was very sick, and would spend the first seven months of her precarious life in the neonatal intensive care unit fighting to stay alive.

During this time, Jim and Margaret Jordan and their children, Alex and Clara, were living in Calgary, Alberta. Jim had begun work with Special Olympics Canada in 1985 as the director of the National Games, to be held in Calgary in the summer of 1986.

If you believe in fate, destiny, kismet, or any of those cosmic forces that seem to bring humans and circumstances together with perfect alignment, then here is where the perfect plan was conceived.

After the Special Olympics National Games were completed, Jim was offered the position of executive director of Special Olympics Ontario. The family moved to Stouffville, Ontario, just north of Toronto. Margaret had been a neonatal nurse in Calgary, but a back injury suffered in 1985 ended her nursing career. Not knowing anyone in her new surroundings, she felt that she didn't have enough to do with just ten-year-old Alex and four-year-old Clara.

Margaret: "One day I was looking in the *Toronto Star* at the weekly feature of 'Friday's Child,' a column that appealed for temporary foster homes for children currently in care at Sick Children's Hospital. So I decided to call and inquire about the child featured that week. As it turned out, I concluded that we would not be able to consider that particular child, but the person I was speaking to then asked some questions about Jim and me. He asked, 'What do you do?' I answered, 'I'm a pediatric nurse, and my husband works with Special Olympics.' With a very interested 'Ohhh,' he asked if he could call me back with some info about another child. On the second call he proceeded to tell me a little bit about a baby girl, thirteen months old, who needed very experienced nursing care, including around-the-clock oxygen therapy. He asked if that would be a problem for us to have in our home. I called Jim at work to see how he felt about it."

Jim: "Maggie had so much experience in neonatal intensive care that I knew she could handle this very well, so at thirteen months and weighing thirteen pounds, Elizabeth came to us in the spring of 1987. The initial idea was that Maggie would nurse her back to health, and then she would return to her birth family."

Over the next several months, while Elizabeth was in their care, there were supervised visits with her and her birthparents. In the meantime, the Jordan family couldn't help but fall in love with beautiful Lizzie. As the months went by, with Elizabeth's physical health still very fragile, meaning that the option of returning her to her birth family wouldn't result in the best outcome for her, the Jordans brought up the idea of adopting her. Children's Aid was very pleased, and the family began the process of adopting Elizabeth, which included undergoing a home study. Their children, Alex and Clara, were devoted to Elizabeth and completely in favour. After some months of legal manoeuvring and a probationary period of a year, Elizabeth's adoption was finalized legally in 1992.

During Elizabeth's early years, keeping her well physically was an enormous challenge. The Jordan children spent countless hours playing with her and keeping her moving in an effort to develop her strength and motor skills. She was on and off oxygen until she was nine, and was in and out of hospital. At one point she was so sick they feared they would lose her, but Elizabeth's incredible will to live shone through every single setback.

Photo by Chris Hardy.

Elizabeth and
Kate.

Jim: "She was a fighter right from the beginning — she really wanted to live."

Margaret: "I, as a neonatal nurse, was astounded that she spent seven months in the NICU, because normally premature babies spend up to the time of their gestation period that they have missed, which in Lizzie's case was three months. She was subject to so much treatment with oxygen and enormous amounts of medication, but she wouldn't give up."

Another very important factor in the Jordans' commitment as a family to Elizabeth has been their deep and enduring faith. Jim, in fact, was a Catholic priest before working for Special Olympics. He remembers experiences that may have helped prepare him for being a father to Elizabeth.

Jim: "When I was growing up, people with intellectual disabilities were warehoused, not as integrated into society as they are today. A couple I met when I was their parish priest had a severely handicapped child among their seven children. They were an amazing family, and I saw their experiences and enormous challenges up close. Of course, then I didn't know what was down the road. Then being involved in Special Olympics before Lizzie came to us was a further irony — a very happy one."

As Elizabeth got older and her physical condition improved, she became more aware of her limitations, as well as of the extraordinary efforts her family were making on her behalf.

Jim: "One night when Lizzie was very sick, I decided I would stay with her in the family room on the pullout couch. She was burning up. Even being so sick, Lizzie realized that I had to get up for work early the next morning, and she kept saying, 'I'm sorry, Daddy. I'm so sorry, Daddy.'"

When Elizabeth was ten, Jim and Margaret took her to Bloorview MacMillan Centre for some intellectual and cognitive assessments.

Margaret: "We knew there were developmental delays, but when the diagnoses placed Lizzie in the first percentile in IQ, and also concluded that she was affected by Fetal Alcohol Syndrome, we cried and cried in the car before we left."

Again they drew on their faith and strong family values belief system to help them through the next phase of parenting Elizabeth. The years would prove to be particularly challenging.

Elizabeth: "It was a crazy life — out of control."

Jim: "As Lizzie got older she had some issues she had to work through, particularly relating to Margaret. Lizzie was struggling with feelings of separation. She had a fear of bonding but yet a longing to bond, because of traumatic experiences as an infant, and that registered with her. Fortunately we were referred to an excellent psychotherapist who had experience in similar cases. She was a real godsend, and in addition to Maggie and Lizzie going together, we all went as a family."

Elizabeth is the third child in the Jordan family. Younger sister Kate offers her perspective on growing up with Elizabeth.

Kate: "We've all had a very different experiences, but being the youngest, I have spent the most time with Elizabeth. Along with Alex and Clara, I am very close to Lizzie. We have had our ups and downs and shared a room for a really long time. It was interesting, but it's nice to have our own room now [looks at Lizzie] isn't it? We had a rocky relationship at times, and I would even say it was sometimes overwhelming. I think it was hard and very frustrating for Lizzie to see me, her younger sister, surpassing her abilities. She would take it out on me in pretty aggressive ways. [Lizzie nods in agreement] I thought, *How can I deal with this?*"

Jim: "We were concerned. We didn't want Kate to try to bring an adult attitude to this. We said to her if she needed to vent, to vent."

Kate: "Even when all of this was going on, I never felt that I wasn't getting the attention or recognition from my parents that I deserved. I was involved in activities like horseback riding and dance, and decided not to become actively involved as a volunteer in Special Olympics. But now I realize that I have been personally inspired by Elizabeth, to the degree that I am working on an Early Childhood Education degree with the intention of working with special-needs children."

At this point in our discussions, the Jordan family is sitting in close quarters on the sofa, Elizabeth sandwiched quite happily between Margaret and Kate. The family dog, Roxy, has held court on Elizabeth's lap for the entire time. I can see the enormous love and pride her parents and sister have for her, and Elizabeth has for them, as she often holds a hand or nuzzles her head on a shoulder.

Photo by Chris Hardy.

Jim, Margaret,
and Elizabeth.

Jim's career, including a fifteen-year tenure as president of Special Olympics Canada and now president of Special Olympics Foundation, has been wonderful for Elizabeth. The list of sports she has participated in is nothing less than impressive.

Elizabeth: "When I was twelve, I won a gold, silver, and bronze medal in speed skating at the provincial winter games." (Jim adds that her three years in house league hockey were good preparation.)

Elizabeth has travelled in Ontario to places like Peterborough, Belleville, and Timmins while com-

Photo by Chris Hardy.

peting in sports such as curling, swimming, and soccer. In 2006 she represented Ontario as a bowler at the National Summer Games in Brandon, Manitoba. Recently she was in Halifax with Jim and Margaret, and together they spoke at a Special Olympics event. Aside from these events, Elizabeth leads a very active life back at home.

Jim: "The real value for Lizzie and others in Special Olympics is in the weekly training with her friends and social events. She bowls on Sunday, curls on Monday, and goes to social get-togethers for two hours every Friday night."

But if that's not enough, you can also find Elizabeth volunteering at the local hospital, high school, and veterinary clinic.

Elizabeth: "I clean (but I won't pick up big poop) and hold the animals. Sometimes if they're too sick or getting over an operation I can't, but they let me know if I can touch them." Her love for animals is evident in her affection for Roxy. The two are inseparable, and she enjoys taking Roxy for walks every day.

Elizabeth graduated from high school within her peer group, and Jim proudly recalls the day of her graduation ceremony.

Elizabeth and devoted friend Roxy.

Jim: "One really important quality in Elizabeth that deserves mention was highlighted at her high school graduation. Elizabeth received a special needs certificate and the Jean Vanier award for her entire high school. This award recognizes the student who has demonstrated the greatest compassion and concern for others. We were all extremely proud of her."

Elizabeth is currently participating in a literacy program that teaches the students life skills in an effort to expand her capacity for independence. She is making great progress, and is even beginning to navigate public transit on her own (cellphone at the ready just in case). It is reassuring to Jim and Margaret that everyone in the community knows Elizabeth and would jump in to help if she needed it.

Elizabeth will continue in the literacy program for as long as she is progressing. There are aspects of her future that are uncertain, depending on what she is capable of and, more importantly, what she wishes to do. She knows she has many guardian angels — the main ones being her parents and her sisters and brother. She becomes visibly distressed when the thought of being without her parents registers with her.

Elizabeth: "What will I do when you guys are gone? Who's going to look after me?"

Margaret: "Your sisters and brother."

Elizabeth: "What happens if they die? I'm afraid of losing you guys!"

Jim and Margaret gently reassure Elizabeth that besides her immediate family, she has a big extended family in Calgary who would never let her be abandoned.

I sit in admiration and respect for the Jordan family. To me they represent the best of humanity. I ask them in summary to express how they are navigating this experience with such grace and humility.

Jim: "Part of it has been our strong faith, certainly, but this is life, you've got to live it — it's not scripted for you."

Margaret: "It's like having your own birth child, there is no difference — you don't know what's going to come through the door. You embrace it, be thankful for it, because it's wonderful — and you look after your child no matter what!"

Elizabeth has found her way to the home and family with which she was meant to be. She is, however, still hopeful that one day she will meet her birthmother — "I really would like to say thank you to her."

Photo by Daniel St. Louis.

The greatest gift of family life is to be intimately acquainted with people you might never introduce yourself to, had life not done it for you.

Kendall Hailey

Open Hearts

The Brown/Wingrove, Wannan, and Foley Families
Toronto, Ontario, and Peterborough, Ontario

"As I held her for the first time, I whispered in her ear that no matter how far apart we are, we will always be together."
— Ryan Foley, birthfather of Kate

ADOPTION BRINGS PEOPLE together, both families and friends. Sometimes they come into your life after years of hoping, and usually they show up unexpectedly. Marj Wingrove came into my life in another one of those chance connections that have enriched my life like a gift for no occasion. We all know women love to share with other women, if only because they know they won't be faced with blank stares. Marj and I met on an adoption website amongst tales of grief and woe. Her posts stood out because I felt she had great common sense, compassion, and humour in just the right amounts. We corresponded, and then we finally met in person when I offered to help her pack boxes for her move out of my neighbourhood back to Toronto. It was a sad and happy day: happy to have met her, sad at her going. We have adoption in common, and a similar philosophy about open adoptions in particular. She and her husband, Felix Brown, are finding their way in one and, in doing so, have opened their hearts to one of their children's birth families.

Their journey began in the fall of 2001, when Marj, tired of infertility treatments and having suffered two ectopic pregnancies, decided it was time to pursue adoption.

Marj: "Felix and I went to an intake meeting and signed on to the list for taking the adoption preparation course. It was more a more serious endeavour for me than for Felix at the time."

Felix: "I thought of adoption as Plan B … not really considering seriously that Plan A would fail."

Marj: "We agreed to let it sit over Christmas, and the following day Felix got a phone call from CAS saying we could start the adoption course in January 2002. It was a seven-week course [now it is a total of twenty-seven hours] for two hours a week, and it was very helpful. It got me thinking about lots of scenarios, like interracial adoption, single and gay adoption. We didn't talk about openness that much until our social worker discussed it with us. At that time I thought you'd have to be crazy to have an open adoption."

Felix: "We were very lucky to have a wonderful and very hardworking social worker and also had great experiences with Toronto CAS, they were always supportive and kind."

Marj: "By June the same year, our home study and all the paperwork was complete, so I decided to do some work in Atlantic Canada over the summer. It was exactly what I needed to clear my mind. When I returned, we signed up for other workshops, one of which was with Jennie Painter in Kingston. We decided since we were so close to Ottawa that we'd go and meet an adoption practitioner there. We barely had our bums in the chair when she put a piece of paper in front of us and said, 'What do you think of this little guy?' She didn't show us a picture of him until after she had told us all about him. After she finished interviewing us, she said, 'Let me know by Thursday if you want to be presented.' I said to Felix as we drove away, 'What if this is our son?'"

The three-month-old-baby had been in foster care since he was two days old, and his birthmother was about to relinquish her parental rights.

Felix: "I'm not a person who can look at a baby's picture and say, 'That's a cute kid' — they all look pretty scrunchy and weird to me — but I thought, *Who is this kid*? We went through his profile with a fine-tooth comb, and there were a few concerns for us both to consider."

Marj: "I don't think I got dressed that week, but basically lived in pajamas while on the Internet and phone, researching … and all the while already picturing him in our lives. I remember that I was ironing when the practitioner called a week later to tell us we'd been chosen. She said, 'Call Felix.' I walked around the house for I don't know how long, and when I finally called him, I could not speak … but it was clear to him what had happened."

It was about eleven months from the time the couple had started the adoption process, which by some standards is not that long; and while she is grateful that it wasn't any longer, Marj emphatically expresses how excruciating those months were.

Marj: "I will tell anyone who asks me that the waiting is the absolute hardest part of all — harder than going through infertility treatments, harder than waiting for approval. You know that it is going to happen, but you don't know who it's going to be; the suspense is so thick."

The couple let the adoption practitioner know the next day that they wanted to proceed with adopting beautiful Reilly. They bought a crib on Saturday and met their new son the following Tuesday.

Marj: "We spent four days with Reilly and his amazing foster mother and brought him home on November 1. When we drove away with him, we looked out of the back window with expectations that someone would surely be following us. We thought, *They're actually going to let us get away with this baby!*"

I ask the couple how their transition to parenthood, and Reilly's transition to them, went.

Marj: "It was easy and beautiful. We had planned to be quiet at first, but our house was full of relatives soon after he came. Reilly was good … he seemed to adjust well."

Felix: "Reilly had a terrible cold when he came home, and he wanted to be carried and comforted a lot, which was helpful in bonding with him. We certainly felt bonded very quickly. During the first few weeks, he seemed to be looking around for someone (his foster mother, no doubt). This was the only thing that was outwardly visible as evidence of some concern … but it didn't continue."

Marj: "It was quite a long time before I felt like I was a mother. When I was at playgroups or at the park, all the other mothers were talking about their pregnancies and deliveries, which made me feel like a fraud. There is such a thing as post-adoption blues, and I felt it. I had accomplished what I set out to do, but I didn't feel entitled to it. Infertility has so much to do with adoption because for some it is their second choice. The first thing is the law of nature, creating a child. But with me, if you put a baby in my arms and tell me it's mine, I'll believe you and look after that baby. Not everyone thinks like that."

Felix: "Most people have the desire to continue their genetic family; that's a big push for many, and truthfully it was a tough transition for me to give that up. It was also difficult to take on the role as Reilly's father once he came home. Logically, everything was there, but emotionally it took a while to let that settle in. After a few months I began to see the person that was in that baby, and it was impossible not to fall in love with Reilly."

Marj and Felix were able to meet Reilly's birthmother and a biological half-sister, who is four years his senior, when Reilly was just over a year old. They could see the family resemblance immediately.

Marj: "Reilly's birthmother was very nervous, but so happy to see him. There was definitely a lot of some form of love in the room. I realized that we all have a role in his life — I can only describe the experience as sacred. We spent two hours together and have since sent letters to her through the adoption practitioner, but sadly she has not picked them up. I am still very hopeful that she will want to reconnect with Reilly and with us. I think he would enjoy meeting his extended family as well."

When Reilly was eighteen months old, Marj and Felix updated their home study and started making adoption inquiries again. In 2004, they were contacted about another little boy who was in care with Reilly's foster mother. This situation and a few others did not materialize as they rode the roller coaster of emotions that make up adoption. However, it may have been due to a higher plan: about four months later, Marj's mother became very ill, and they put their plans on hold while Marj devoted her time to her mom before her passing. It was not until early 2006 that Marj and Felix began letting themselves hope again. They were about to learn about open adoption and what it would mean to their family.

A birthmother's social worker called to tell them that her client was considering them as potential adoptive parents and wanted to meet them.

Marj and Felix met twenty-one-year-old Kayley Wannan and her mother at their home in Peterborough. Her baby's birthfather, Ryan Foley, was not present at their initial meeting.

Kaley: "I was scared and I didn't know what to do. I thought that if I kept it out of my mind, then maybe it would go away. I made countless appointments to have an abortion, but in the end just couldn't go through with it. I also knew that I couldn't raise a baby. I kept asking myself, 'Why is this happening to me?' — and then it occurred to me that every day others were waking up wondering the same thing. It made sense from that point. Then I met Marj, Felix, and Reilly."

Photo by Daniel St. Louis.

Kayley, Marj, Kate, Felix, and Ryan.

Kayley and Ryan, Ryan's parents, Jane and Tom, and Ryan's sister, Laura, are gathered in the living area of Marj and Felix's home on a quiet street off the Danforth in Toronto. Two-year-old Kate is happily toddling around, enjoying morsels from a snack plate, and taking short cuddle breaks with eager family members. Six-year-old Reilly is there too, and perhaps has an inkling of the still raw emotions of our conversation around his sister's adoption. I can see the complexities of feelings on the faces of this family — birth family and adoptive family — as they share their experiences. It is heart-rending. Kate's birthfather, Ryan, is visibly conflicted as he recounts his memory of the months and days before his daughter's birth.

Ryan: "I wanted very badly to raise Kate any way that I could. I spoke with a social worker, who told me that I would never get custody on my own. When Kayley kept making

118

appointments to have an abortion, I didn't know where to turn. Kayley's mom was encouraging her to have one, so she and I were not speaking. Kayley thought her mom was going to kick her out of the house."

Kayley: "I was being told different things by everyone, and I felt helpless. Once I had Kate and had made the decision to place her with Marj and Felix, my mom accepted the decision and was sorry about her first reactions to our situation."

Ryan: "Rationally I knew that I couldn't raise Kate on my own, and

Photo by Daniel St. Louis.

Grandad Tom.

Kayley and her mom were not prepared to do it. I kept telling myself that if I let Kate go now, I'd never be able to get her back. I felt sick and anxious every day before her birth, not knowing what would happen. My parents were there if I wanted them, but at the time I was angry at them … and at everyone, for not helping me. I felt alone."

Tom (Ryan's father): "Before we met Marj and Felix, I already felt encouraged about the idea, because they had already adopted Reilly; I thought they must be a good family."

Jane (Ryan's mother): "Initially I was very anxious about the idea of adoption, because you hear the stories about kids in foster care — but when I met Marj and Felix I felt good about them."

Kayley adds: "The first thing that I liked about them was that they seemed understanding — not judgmental. Marj is hip (I saw her nose piercing) and I knew I'd be able to talk to her openly and that if there were ever difficult times she would be willing to listen and understand."

Felix: "The last few weeks before Kate's birth were the most stressful. I knew about

Ryan's efforts to be a father to Kate — he was understandably fighting for his offspring, and the prospect of meeting him in court was not something I was willing to do. I thought, where would that leave us afterwards? There would be no hope of having a relationship in the future. The stakes were too high."

Marj: "When Kate was born on February 28, 2006, we were staying at my sister's in Peterborough [Kayley's hometown], and Felix and I waited at the hospital. Kayley's mother and aunt were with her during Kate's delivery, but Ryan by that time was considered a security risk, and measures were taken to prevent him from going in to the hospital. After Kate was born, Felix and I were invited to go and see her in the nursery. We didn't see Kayley until the evening after Kate was born, and only by accident. She was outside of the hospital taking a break, in her robe and sitting in a wheelchair. We had a really casual, relaxed conversation — just us — no one was bugging us or knowing our business. That was a very pivotal meeting, and I feel lucky we had that, because it set the tone for the relationship that we share today. The next evening (before Kate was to go into foster care) when we met again, Kayley wanted to talk about naming the baby. She is named after my mother, Katherine, who would have adored her new granddaughter had she had the opportunity."

Kayley: "I was happy that Marj and Felix were at the hospital so that they could bond with Kate right away. I didn't know if I wanted to see Kate — I wondered what that would be like for me.

Photo by Daniel St. Louis.

Aunt Laura, Reilly, and Grandma Jane.

I knew that Ryan and his family wanted to have contact. My mom told me that she would meet Kate when I was ready to. I needed to give myself time to see what it was like after I had her."

Ryan saw Kate the day after her birth, accompanied by his parents and a close friend.

Ryan: "I saw Kate every day from when she was born until she left the hospital. As I held her for the first time, I whispered in her ear that no matter how far apart we are, we will always be together."

Marj: "We met Ryan's parents, Jane and Tom, at the hospital. We knew and were happy that they wanted to be grandparents, but we didn't know what that meant yet. They were relieved, I think, that we were so willing to be open to the degree that they would know Kate. Nobody could have predicted that we would be this close to them — so open."

I ask Tom and Jane about those first awkward moments and days.

Jane: "At first I was so concerned because I didn't know Marj and Felix. My first thought of Marj was 'My God, she's got a nose ring!' It wasn't that I didn't want the adoption, and I knew that Kate needed it, but Kate is my first grandchild. It felt in one way that we had lost her — but not really. She would not be a part of us in the way that we hoped she'd be. My close girlfriend was the one that got me through it. She's been there for me through the tough times."

Tom: "I didn't have as hard a time as Jane. I tried to look at it more rationally — that everything would work out for the better. My mother thought it was just great that there was another adopted child [Reilly] in their family because they would be able to relate to each other in a very important way."

Kate was in the hospital for four days after her birth and then in foster care in Toronto for three weeks. It was a very uncomfortable situation and a dramatic time.

Marj: "I went almost every day, got to hold Kate for an hour, and [was] then encouraged to leave. I really had some concerns about how she was being cared for and called our social worker and the licensee to express my concerns. Even though Ryan had not signed the final adoption papers [Kayley had] we were thankfully able to bring Kate home."

Photo by Daniel St. Louis.

Mom to mom.

121

Photo by Daniel St. Louis.

Kiss for Kate.

Ryan: "The last time I saw Kate before she left the hospital, I felt numb and walked home by myself. I didn't want to talk to anyone. I stayed to myself. I had never felt like that before. I went to the lawyers two or three times before I finally could sign the adoption papers. It was the hardest decision of my life."

Marj and Felix's adoption of Kate is a family relationship in progress. It is not without its challenges, but everyone is keeping beautiful Kate and her brother, Reilly, at the centre of the journey. Ryan's extended family members have embraced Kate's adoptive family from the beginning.

Jane: "We consider Reilly as our grandson and enjoy our relationship with him immensely. He has stayed at our home a few times, and it's wonderful to know that Kate has him as her big brother."

Tom: "It was important that our family feel about Reilly as they do about Kate. He is always included during gift giving occasions and celebrations. Reilly is a part of our family too."

Marj: "At the start we made more formal arrangements for getting together. It was a little strained, and we all wondered where it would go. It's sometimes a challenge when situations arise that might be conflicting, just like it is with all families. I've made it my policy not to try to guess what they're thinking. But we didn't have this with Reilly's adoption, so it is wonderful for him to have so much family around, in addition to Felix's and mine. Adoption brings a different kind of family. Since both my parents are gone, I appreciate that our kids have more grandparents through this openness. Sometimes I wonder how we have had the good fortune of these loving people turning up in our lives. Then I remind myself that it doesn't matter how we all came together, we respect and love each other … just because …"

I ask Kate's birth family what it feels like being welcomed into Marj and Felix's home.

Tom: "You can tell when you walk into their home that it's a loving one, just by how the kids react. And you know what Marj and Felix are like by the fact that they invited Ryan to stay here overnight — that tells you something. I'm sure quite a few people would think that's odd. But people really need to understand what open adoption is. I have a co-worker who, after I told her about our relationship, thought it was great. Her daughter was facing the same dilemma, and she was wishing she would consider adoption for her baby."

Ryan: "It's becoming more comfortable. To me the house itself doesn't matter so much. It's what is going on inside that counts. Their values were my first concern. When I came, Kate took me by the hand and [led me] up the stairs to show me her room. I have kept every email that Marj and I have corresponded with, and I go back and reread them."

Kayley: "When I first met Kate, it was very emotional. To see her so happy and loved helps me to realize that I had made the right decision for both of us. I will always be a part of her life,

Photo by Daniel St. Louis.

Kate's eyes are on lunch.

and that gives me peace of mind. I'm so thankful that I gave her life and adoption instead of the alternative. Marj, Felix, Reilly, and Kate are family to me, and I am grateful every day for that."

Jane: "For me, the hardest part is not being close enough physically. My friends who have grandchildren are able to see them more easily, kind of drop in on them anytime. I miss that part of it."

Marj: "I miss that too."

Ryan: "Marj and Felix have been great … very accommodating to our family. We all are happy to have full contact — the best part is being able to be a part of Kate growing up. I wouldn't have agreed to do this any other way. Nothing else matters as long as Kate is happy. I look forward to the day when she can call me up and tell me how her day was."

Marj looks ahead to the future with her own thoughts and says, "When she gets married you'll be in the front pews, right? This family's always going to be our family."

At this point I turn my gaze to Kayley, who is shedding some tears (as we all are). I ask her quietly, "You know it was a good decision, right?"

She answers, "Yes, yes it was — I can't help thinking about the other choice I could have made …"

And I say, "But you didn't … you didn't."

It has been an extraordinary afternoon. I have had the privilege of sharing in the moments of two families who have made difficult but life-affirming choices — painful, yes, but for the future of a precious little girl name Kate. She is, and will always be, well loved.

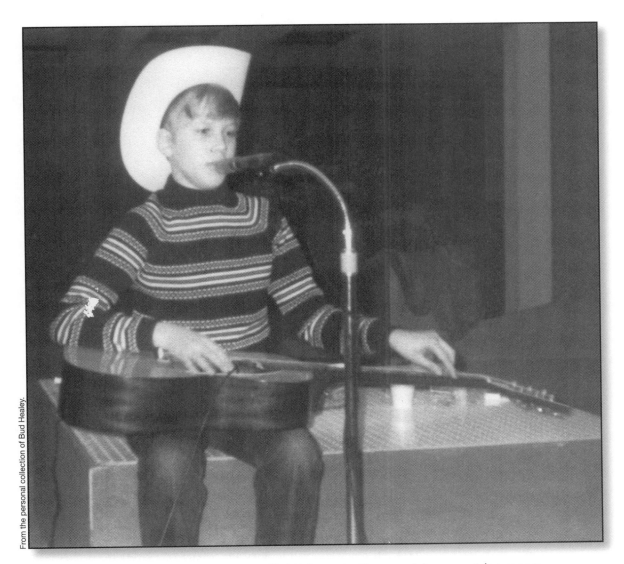

From the personal collection of Bud Healey.

The best and most beautiful things in the world cannot be seen
or even touched — they must be felt with the heart.

Helen Keller

Perfect Harmony
Jeff Healey
Toronto, Ontario

"I just thought that was how you got kids:
made a phone call, talked to someone, and ordered one."
— Jeff Healey

When I interviewed Jeff Healey in the spring of 2007, I knew he was facing some challenges with the spread of tumours related to retinoblastoma. He was optimistic, upbeat, and determined to continue with his life's passions: family, friends, and music. It was with profound sadness that I learned of Jeff's death on March 2, 2008. Selfishly, I had looked forward to seeing him again, as I found him to be an extraordinary man. His music will live on forever, but the quiet and impassioned words he shared with me during my privileged time with him about his greatest gifts — his children and his family — will resonate with me as long as I live. Following are the perspectives he wanted to share with you. Thank you, Jeff.

WHEN YOU HEAR the name Jeff Healey, you think about one of Canada's most celebrated and accomplished musicians. For more than twenty-five years, Jeff gave us a wide range of musical genres from which to choose. In addition to his many Juno and Gemini award nominations, in June 2004 Jeff received an honorary Doctorate of Letters from McMaster University in Hamilton. In November 2007 he was also awarded an honorary licentiate by the Conservatory of Canada.

What makes his success more remarkable is that Jeff was blind from the age of one, as a result of retinoblastoma, a childhood cancer of the eye. As I drive into his quiet Toronto neighbourhood, I am struck by how ordinary it seems, but I expect that our conversation about his adoption will be anything but.

Jeff answers the door, towering over me while trying to keep his balance. There is an adorable little blond version of him wrapped around one leg. Two-year-old Derek is hanging on for dear life. Their mutual adoration is evident. After I meet Jeff's wife, Cristie, we descend to a room that is almost a museum. I am privileged to be surrounded by Jeff's carefully stored and catalogued extensive record collection. According to his father, Bud, Jeff can pick any record out from one of the divided custom-built shelves that line the four walls and tell you its name and the songs that are on each side. Bud and I speak separately about his life as Jeff Healey's father. Jeff's mother, Yvonne, passed away in 1994.

From the personal collection of Bud Healey.

Jeff's birth family were wealthy Hamiltonians, and he was the third child born to his birthmother, a result of a sporadic relationship with a much older married man. He was placed in foster care until he was three months old, at precisely the same time Bud and Yvonne Healey wanted to adopt a baby boy. They had applied with Children's Aid in Toronto and were at their cottage when they received the call. Were they interested in considering a three-month-old boy? The day after meeting him, they brought him home to the apartment where they would live until he was three.

Bud's profession as a firefighter took him away for long hours, but when he came home from work, he and Jeff developed a routine of playtime: "Jeff would sit on my stomach, and we would fool around or eat a snack together. One day I noticed that he was only reaching out to one side of my face. We took him to a specialist at Sick Children's Hospital, who gave us the shocking news. Jeff had retinoblastoma: pediatric eye cancer."

A happy Yvonne with baby Jeff.

Jeff: "I was four and half months old and still in the probationary period of my adoption, so they easily could have sent me back."

Bud: "It never entered our minds."

Jeff: "They went above and beyond the call of duty in looking after me and getting me the proper treatment."

Bud: "Because we were still in the trial period, all the medical decisions had to be approved by the Children's Aid. Technically, they were his guardians still. That really bothered me; this was my kid, and I didn't have the authority to give the doctors consent."

By his first birthday, Jeff's eyes had been removed, and he was fitted with prosthetic ones.

From the personal collection of Bud Healey.

Mother and son bond
ever close.

Bud: "It was a shock, and it changed our whole way of trying to make things work, but Jeff did so well. As soon as he walked, he was doing everything that every other kid was doing. The layout of the apartment was imprinted in his mind. Yvonne was a stay-at-home mom, so they became very close."

Jeff: "When I was three or four I remember telling Mrs. Upton, our social worker, that I wanted a sister and that I was going to call her Linda. One day at our cottage, someone came over on the boat from the general store (we had no phone) to tell us there was a message from Children's Aid. It was September 1970. They were offering twin girls, and my parents decided to go with it. At the office, one baby sat on Dad's lap and the other on my mother's. I put a hand on each of their heads and said, 'This is Linda and this is Laura.' Growing up, we always knew we were adopted, and I just thought that was how you got kids: made a phone call, talked to someone, and ordered one."

Jeff's extended family on both sides was large, and the children were welcomed with open arms. He was particularly close to his grandmothers, one of whom is still living at ninety-five. There were spiritual influences of both Baptist and United Church faiths.

Jeff: "I was so fortunate to have two of the best ladies one could have as grandmothers. They instilled in me that one needs some sort of belief system. If I ever had any doubts about the benefits of religion, all I have to do is look to my grandmothers — it must work for something."

As a boy, Jeff proved to be very bright while attending the Ross McDonald School for the Blind in Brantford, Ontario. His love and aptitude for music surfaced very early on.

Bud: "He would listen to our hi-fi, particularly jazz and Broadway musical songs — all the music our family listened to. By three, he was learning to play the guitar, piano, and then the trombone and trumpet at Brantford. As a teenager, he was so talented, but I was worried about how he could support himself in music. Because of his incredible knowledge retention and photographic memory, I felt he could have been an excellent lawyer."

We are fortunate that Jeff's heart was in music, and there it always remained.

The subject of adoption came to the surface more as Jeff and his sisters approached their twenties.

Bud: "We had no problem with the idea of the children having a relationship with their birth families. The girls did meet their birthfather, but a relationship did not materialize."

Jeff: "When I had my daughter, I felt compelled to learn more about my birth family for medical reasons. I was learning more about retinoblastoma and its hereditary patterns. My birth name — Brian Alan Moodie — was on some documents I had, and after some detective work, I managed to find my birthmother. My first conversation with her was very emotional; in fact, she said I had the wrong number and hung up. A few days later she called back and we spoke. Clearly, she was deathly afraid of her family finding out about me. Prior to me, she had given birth to a baby girl, my full sibling, whom she had kept. I tried to get across to her that she had to find a way to tell her daughter about my cancer. Both she and her children needed to be checked for the gene. As far as I know, it still has not happened."

Jeff has not spoken to his birthmother since 2001, but there are times when he still feels emotionally overcome with his desire to inform his sister of the information she is entitled to know.

Jeff: "I was never looking for another mother or another sister. I was raised in a very close family and have so many friends. Mine is a rich life. But somewhere there is a lady that needs to know and her kids need to know. I've done what I can do."

Jeff's first child, Rachel, now thirteen, does not have the gene for retinoblastoma, but unfortunately three-year-old Derek does. He is being treated by Dr. Brenda Gallie at Toronto Sick Children's Hospital. She is the leading research physician in Canada for this particular cancer. There are still no definitive answers as to how it starts and why. Jeff was involved in the research to find a cure, with Derek at the top of his mind, along with many other children he has met over the years. The work will continue.

From the personal collection of Bud Healey.

Bud and Jeff.

Bud: "Jeff and the girls grew up like they were our own children. I was not affected in a negative way at all by the fact that our family was formed by adoption. Not every adopted child is rejected. Birthparents who place their children want the best for them. People now seem so hung up on having a biological child, when there are so many children out there who need a home. And you can do that so easily — give a child a home and be a parent."

Jeff doesn't recall suffering any stigma as a child around being adopted.

Jeff: "My mother told me if I ever got teased, that I should tell kids that they chose me."

When Jeff was twenty-eight, his beloved mother, Yvonne, succumbed to breast cancer. She was only fifty-five. Jeff was grateful for her strong influence in helping him develop his sense of self and his place in the world.

Jeff: "My mother and grandmothers believe that I'm this special person who was put on this earth, different from the rest, for special reasons. Whatever I wanted to do, they defended and supported me. I always felt loved and cherished. And now I have two wonderful kids who mean more to me than anything else in the world. I'm hoping that I am thought of by both of my wives as being a first-rate father, which I never figured I could be. It happened by default, really. I love my children to such a degree … they are the two blood relatives that are close to me. I see so much of me in both of them. My daughter at thirteen wants to be her own person, but recognizes when she does something that's very much like her dad. My son is me all over again, watching him at this age. He's very musical, in tune with everything, and doesn't miss a thing — just a happy, loving little boy. Conversely, my parents no doubt wondered where traits of mine come from. I was singing adult songs, playing instruments, and talking about bits of music history at three. They must have thought, *What is this freak we adopted?*"

So Jeff was left to wonder as well, but he did not linger over the missing details of his birth families. Unfortunately, there is a woman who cannot bring herself to acknowledge him as her son, thereby putting her daughter and grandchildren at potential risk.

Bud and his current wife, Rose, attended as many of Jeff's performances as possible, and over the years they made an interesting observation. Quite often they would notice a particular woman, always by herself, walking around. She is of an age that raises questions about her identity. Could she be Jeff's birthmother? If his birthmother is ambivalent about her decision, that emotion has no place in Jeff's heart.

Jeff: "I can say completely and to the end of my days that concerning my life, everything that has happened has happened for a reason. I was born and put here in the world for a reason. The people who by the grace of God were supposed to take care of me adopted me. They were smart enough to recognize my health problems and get the help I needed. So I can very easily and justifiably say that adoption was the right thing for me."

Jeff Healey's story emphasizes the importance of disclosure, at the very least with regards to medical history. It can literally be a matter of life and death.

I was honoured to be invited to be present at Jeff's funeral service at a church he had joined with his family. The service was a moving tribute to Jeff's talent as a musician, his commitment to friendships, and his devotion to his family. The presiding minister included in the service a verse that I felt was particularly apropos, and somehow comforting, in the midst of such deep sadness. The verse comes from a hymn that was written by Robert Lowry in 1860 entitled "How Can I Keep from Singing."

My life flows on in endless song;
Above earth's lamentation
I hear the sweet though far off hymn
That hails a new creation:
Through all the tumult and the strife
I hear the music ringing;
It finds an echo in my soul —
How can I keep from singing?

Photo by Chris Hardy.

The tie that links mother and child is of such
pure and immaculate strength as to be never violated.

Washington Irving

Finding Diana
The Brennan Family
Oakville, Ontario

"When I went home that night, I just curled up in my bed, and I think I stayed like that for three days."
— Artrina Heinbecker, birthmother of Diana

ADOPTION ISN'T A one-time event — it is a journey that begins with the inkling of an idea surrounding the desire to be a parent. I have not met anyone who chose to adopt without having first considered creating a child biologically, but I am sure they are out there, and it would be good to meet them.

My husband, Dave, and I married in our mid-thirties and were blessed by the birth of our son, Daniel, in 1993. I was thirty-eight, Dave thirty-six. We naturally assumed we would have another child, as we felt strongly about the importance of a sibling for our son. When complications arose with a second pregnancy that ultimately resulted in a miscarriage, we decided to pursue adoption in earnest. Our initial inquiries into adoption left us discouraged and frustrated. It seemed that wherever we turned we were told that adopting an infant domestically would be next to impossible because of our age and the fact that we had a biological son. In the later 1990s, most birthmothers placing their babies in adoptive families liked younger, childless, and preferably infertile couples. We considered international adoption but decided that if it were possible, a domestic adoption would give us the opportunity to have an open adoption or at least the option of a connection with the child's birth family.

Despite the dismal predictions of agencies and adoption licensees, we registered with three of them and pondered our next move.

I have never been someone who is able to wait while trying to achieve a goal. In fact, when the stakes are really high I just can't. I learned that we could advertise in newspapers to search for a connection to a potential birthmother, or write letters of introduction to physicians, telling them of our desire to adopt.

Once I felt I could take part in making our goal a reality, it was the most empowering feeling — time was not on our side, as by 1999 I was almost forty-four. Placing our ad in college and university newspapers as well as others in Ontario gave me pause. My conservative nature was being shattered once and for all. I think Dave must have wondered if I had lost my mind. I wondered if I had lost my mind.

Dave and I had two great professional supporters who helped to guide us — Donna Novosel, the social worker who got to know us through doing our home study, and JoAnne Conlin, who assisted us throughout. JoAnne was adamant in her belief in me and her belief that the predictions others had made regarding our chances had nothing to do with my resolve to make it happen. We also received support from our families and friends. My sister Kathy was instrumental in providing encouragement and Kleenex when I needed it. I placed the ads in the papers in February, not knowing that the baby we would adopt had already been conceived.

Artrina Heinbecker was sixteen when she discovered she was pregnant. She knew there were three options to consider — abortion, parenting, or adoption. After talking with her sister Davina and realizing neither abortion nor parenting were possibilities for her, Artrina saw the appearance of a little newspaper clipping as a possible answer.

Artrina: "I don't support abortion, and I knew I was not ready to be a parent. My sister was the one who gave me the ad. When I saw it, I thought, *Are you serious? Are these people crazy?* I knew nothing about how you place a baby for adoption — but I did know I didn't want to go through a Children's Aid Society. I think I had the ad for a few weeks before I finally talked with my mom about it. I was surprised that Mom was so calm and understanding about the news. She really took the time to talk about it with me. I told her I didn't want to call the number by myself or meet them alone."

Dave and I had a 1–800 number added to our phone line specifically for the purpose of receiving adoption-related calls. It was nerve-wracking to hear it ring, and after several false alarms the sound of it no longer raised my blood pressure. The day it rang on April 29, 1999, however, meant a lot more to our family than a quickening heartbeat.

Artrina: "I was so nervous to speak. Because I had already been through feeling so badly and guilty about being pregnant, I was worried about what this couple would think of me. Would they think I was a bad person because of this — were they going to judge me only because of this?"

When I answered the phone that day I was not prepared for what would happen next. I had been about to take five-year-old Daniel to a birthday party, but the party would have to wait. I remember speaking to Artrina's mother, Jan, first, and then Artrina's quiet and nervous voice came on the phone. I felt for her — a sixteen-year-old facing such a momentous decision. I felt compelled to ask her about the two things that others felt would be obstacles to our goal. Artrina thought our age meant maturity and stability, and a big brother for her baby was a big advantage. I heaved a huge sigh of relief and, without getting a phone number from Artrina, headed off to the birthday party in a state of numbed disbelief.

Artrina: "After I spoke with Debbie, I felt very calm. I wanted to meet them and I told her I'd call her in a week. My sister Davina had just had a baby girl, and I spent three days with her seeing first-hand the reality of caring for a newborn. It was then I truly realized that I was not cut out to be a mom yet. Had my niece Elaine not been born, I might have reconsidered."

More than a week went by, and I had not heard from Artrina. I was getting very nervous, thinking that I had either dreamed up the entire phone call or she had decided not to proceed. But on the evening of May 12 (my forty-fourth birthday) I received the gift of a lifetime: Artrina called, and we set a date to meet at a local restaurant.

My husband, Dave, recalls, "Before we met, I felt nervous anticipation, not knowing what to expect."

I was a bundle of nerves, but after two hours of conversation about everything but the reason we had all gathered, I just had to bring up adoption. Dave, Artrina, and Artrina's mother, Jan, almost made me feel like I was interrupting their party. I asked Artrina if she had any questions for us about anything. She answered that she had just one: "Are you going to stay home with the baby and not work?" Without hesitation I said yes. We left the restaurant filled with excited anticipation. Artrina's baby was due in just over four months. In some ways it would feel like a long time, but in others, it was a blessing.

JoAnne Conlin became involved in the process, and a social worker, Luvia Treflin, became Artrina's source of information and support.

Artrina: "She was a really sweet lady and did a very good job of giving me all the options for both adoption and parenting. She was there for me, for what I needed and wanted. She gave me every opportunity to consider other couples or to keep my baby. I was confident with my plan — I had no doubts."

Dave: "After we met Artrina until just before Diana was born, I felt concerned that Artrina might change her plan for us to adopt her baby. Not long before her due date of September 23, we met her again with our prospective social workers and her mother. I remember Artrina reaching across the table and touching Deb's arm, saying that she wanted her to be in the delivery room and cut her baby's cord. We all cried with the realization of the magnitude of Artrina's decision."

There was one false labour alarm before the big day, and I spent the day with Artrina as she laboured. Davina was there with her baby, Elaine, and Jan was there in time to see her daughter deliver her second granddaughter. It was amazing to experience Diana's birth. She was tiny (six pounds, two ounces) and perfect, and under my attempt at being respectfully controlled, I was jumping for joy. After gazing at her for a few minutes, I excused myself and ran down the hall to call Dave and Daniel to say, "It's a girl!"

The experience of having given birth to Daniel gave me an odd perspective on the moment of Diana's birth. I felt such empathy for Artrina, such sadness at the decision she was facing, and yet such happiness at the prospect of us having a daughter and Daniel having a sister. I felt that Artrina needed to spend time with her baby; as a mother, I needed her to be sure, so I was determined to try to stay away to let her have that precious time.

The night that Dave and I went back to the hospital to bring Diana home was probably the most emotional one for all of us. Artrina's mother and social worker were there as we awk-

Photo by Chris Hardy.

Artrina, Diana, and
Deborah.

wardly anticipated what was about to take place. Here was this beautiful and perfect baby girl, with her mother, and here were we, about to become parents again in a very different context than the first time. I asked for some private moments with Artrina as she sat on the bed holding her baby. I looked into her eyes and told her that if she wasn't sure about her decision that Diana could go into foster care for the time being. Artrina told me she was very sure of her decision and that she wanted us to take her baby home with us. I asked her how she was so sure. She quietly said, "Because I know I will see her again."

Dave: "I remember we got to the hospital at 7:30 p.m., and at 9:30 Artrina's social worker got on her feet and said, 'It's time to go.' Artrina's mom put her arm around her as she walked over to Deb and handed Diana off to her without a word. She turned and walked out the door with her mom on one side and her social worker on the other. Deb and I were a blubbering mess. Our social worker, Donna, told us we needed to sit down. I had such feeling for Artrina — for what she had just endured and was still going through — and then, in the next second, pure jubilation for this beautiful baby girl."

Starting that night, it was a surreal experience. We went down to the same van we had brought Daniel home in and looked at each other in disbelief that she was coming home with us. I felt like we were kidnapping her. Daniel was waiting for us, a very excited six-year-old meeting his new baby sister. That night I slept on my back with six-pound Diana nestled in on my chest. It was the first time in my life I had felt deep sadness and exhilarating joy at the same time.

Artrina: "When I went home that night, I just curled up in a ball on my bed, and I think I stayed like that for three days. Everyone took care of me because I was emotionally and physically in pain and exhausted. I didn't want to deal with anything. I thought, *Am I ever going to feel normal again?*"

We thought about Artrina every day as we settled into life with Diana. Our family and friends were so excited and happy to see her. I had heard and read about entrustment ceremonies, and I felt that it would be a way to honour Artrina and the courage she had shown. When Diana was five weeks old, we held the ceremony in the chapel of my mother's church. (See Appendix A.) It was very emotional and bittersweet, but I think a confirmation of our commitment as a family to Artrina and the baby girl she had placed in our care.

After the entrustment ceremony, we didn't see Artrina again until Diana was a year old, and then only for a short time. When she was two we saw her again, while in between visits we sent letters and photographs. The visits took place in neutral locations, something that made for neutral emotions, although Artrina admits how hard it was to walk away after seeing Diana.

Artrina: "I have never regretted the decision I made, but it was always hard during the first year to walk away; that's why I think I had to go to live elsewhere. I didn't want it to be hard; I wanted to enjoy it and be comfortable knowing afterwards that everything was fine — she was loved, well taken care of, and happy — but it was also hard for me to accept that she was all that, but not because of me. I think that's why I went away. I couldn't be the one to make her happy. My mom said, 'You have to go away and deal with you.'"

Artrina moved to Elliott Lake, where her grandmother lives, to distance herself from the pain of coming to terms with the decision to place Diana for adoption.

Artrina: "When I was away from her, I thought about her all the time. I would talk about her as my daughter and that she lived in another home with her parents, trying to explain to people what open adoption was for us. People would look at me like I had two heads."

While Artrina was in Elliott Lake she became pregnant again. I remember getting in touch with her to talk about my hopes of writing this book, when she spoke about the possibility of placing this baby as well. Dave and I were not in a position to adopt again, but since the baby would be a half-sibling to Diana, I was concerned about her placing the baby where Diana would have difficulty keeping connected. Artrina, with the support and counsel of a very close friend named Anne Marie, made the decision to parent this time.

Artrina: "I think my decision to parent Brandon, while very scary, was another one that turned out to be the best decision at that time of my life. Without him, I wouldn't have come back, gone to school, got my driver's licence. It made me realize more than I could have imagined, that placing Diana was an even better decision than I originally thought. In the beginning, I knew it was a good thing for her, but I realized then that it was the best thing for both of us.

"After I had Brandon, and came down and stayed with Deb and Dave, it was great. They knew what they were doing, and it gave me a chance to see how they had been with Diana when she was a baby and what Diana's reaction to my parenting Brandon would be. They stayed with him and helped me, and I think they helped me survive those first six months. It was seeing all of them that nailed it for me. I knew everything would be okay. Seeing Diana and them and seeing how they were together, I knew I had nothing to worry about. I knew they loved her and would raise her the way that she should be raised."

When Artrina moved back to Hamilton, we were able to see more of her. We got to know her, and we became more comfortable with each other and ready to begin the next phase of our relationship. I was anxious to have Artrina come to our home, although at first there was some apprehension by all of us.

Artrina: "I was nervous because this was your space — your home. I felt like I was invading, but as we talked and it became more comfortable I thought, *They've accepted me as part of their family and they trust that I'm not here to sneak out the back door.*"

Dave: "We got to know you better, on occasions, birthdays, Christmas — it took a while. When I tell people about our story, I always give you credit for your courage. To do what you did, and have the wherewithal and emotional stability to say, 'This is the right thing to do — and I'm going to do it.' For many people it is hard to fathom having a relationship with their child's birthmother. I had no clue what to expect. I'm sure, though it doesn't register with me now, that I had some thoughts about open adoption like, How often are we going to see her around here? … She's here for a week … We'll have to build another room on the house … She's going to show up for Sunday dinner."

I remember hoping that seeing our home — Diana's room, books, toys, and the backyard she plays in — would help Artrina when she did leave. She would at least have a visual of where her daughter was growing up. What didn't make her cry, I hoped would help her heal.

Artrina: "I think the first two to three years after I had Diana were a big emotional blur. I think having

Photo by Chris Hardy.

Deborah, Artrina, Diana, Daniel, and Dave.

Brandon woke me up to really confirming that placing Diana was the absolute right choice. Sometimes when I am exhausted and frustrated with being a mom, I think to myself, *There's no way I could have done this six years ago.* Never once in eight years did I think I made the wrong choice. As I go through all the stages of development with Brandon, I think of what those moments with Diana must have been like."

For us, it is such a positive for Diana to have Artrina, Brandon, and her family be a part of her life. I'm glad Artrina will be there along the way when more in-depth questions will come. I do wish her birthfather would come forward to meet her. He doesn't know what he is missing! She is our great joy along with our son, Daniel. While some will say having a biological child and then adopting is exactly the same, I cannot share that view. While the depth of love, the fierce protectiveness, and the pride is the same, I know that I did not give birth to Diana. She is the miraculous creation of two others. We are grateful to be able to know one of those people, and it is amazing to share the wonder of Diana with the woman who brought her into our world. Our journey will continue together.

141

Artrina: "I still get mixed reactions from people when I tell them our story. Nobody can understand how I can do it. They look at me with a funny expression — but it's so hard to explain it unless you've experienced it. I just knew there was something better for her. It is a great experience. You have to be open to it and be willing to put some effort into it."

Diana turned nine on September 14, 2008. Eight seems to have been an age when questions about her adoption were getting more complicated. As she has known her story from the beginning, seeing Artrina is a matter of fact, but other issues came up. One day she said, "Daniel's not my real brother, is he, Mom?" I asked what she meant by real, and she said, "Well, Daniel came out of your tummy and I came out of Artrina's, so that means he's not my real brother." I said, "Daniel is my biological son and you are Artrina's biological daughter. 'Real' to me means someone who's with you, loves you, protects you, and you can count on. In that way, Daniel is your real brother" — crisis averted. Then came the next zinger: "Mom, sometimes it's weird having two mothers." I asked, "Why's that, Diana?" She answered, "Well, I don't know which one to love the most." As I took a breath, I said, "You know what, Diana, I don't think you need to worry about that at

Photo by Chris Hardy.

all, because we know you love us both, and you don't have to love either one of us more than the other."

Sometimes I get a little nervous, thinking about all that is to come with this miracle called Diana as she grows into a teenager and adult; but mostly I'm very excited because there are no secrets in her life. The word *adoption* in our house won't stand for mystery; it will stand for celebration.

Photo by Daniel St. Louis.

What children take from us, they give … We become people who feel more deeply, question more deeply, hurt more deeply, and love more deeply.
Sonia Taitz, *O Magazine*, May 2003

Take Two

The Smits/McLean Family
Toronto, Ontario

"People have asked, 'How do you feel about them not being your real children?'"
— Seaton McLean

OKAY, I'LL ADMIT it — the prospect of interviewing a Gemini award–winning actress and the former head of film production for Alliance Atlantis has me trying to calm a generous supply of butterflies. I've been a fan of Sonja Smits since I first watched her portray Carrie Barr in *Street Legal*. Not only has she played strong, purposeful, and multi-layered characters, she happens to have done it while being a classically glamorous woman. Now I have the privilege of seeing her in the role she loves best — that of mother to seventeen-year-old Avalon and thirteen-year-old Lian. Sonja and her husband, Seaton McLean, have also added winemaker to their illustrious resumés. Their latest passion is directing their creative energies to Closson Chase Vineyards, a successful winery in Prince Edward County. But that's another story …

As one might imagine, the couple's elegant home reflects their appreciation of the arts, but at the same time it accommodates the needs of their active family and affable dog, a Nova Scotia Duck Toller named Hobbs. One of the first things I hear when I am ushered into their dining room is laughter (always a good sign), and there is plenty more of that as we all get comfortable in the light-filled family room, overlooking a lush back garden.

Sonja and Seaton began to consider adoption to build a family after several years of infertility challenges, including Sonja's suffering two ectopic pregnancies. They had some knowledge of adoption through several of their close friends, as well as Sonja's sister, who had adopted. After contacting the Children's Aid Society, and not being encouraged by that option, they decided to complete a home study privately.

Sonja: "The process of being approved to adopt was surprisingly intense. Potential adoptive parents are under such scrutiny. During the process it struck me that biological parents should undergo a similar assessment before committing to having children."

It was also a time of self-evaluation in terms of deciding what their personal limitations would be. Could they take on a child with special needs? Or a child who had been exposed to drugs or alcohol?

Sonja: "The whole process forces you to very honest about your abilities and your limits. It was a very humbling experience."

They were advised to let people know about their hopes to adopt, including writing letters to various physicians. After a few opportunities that did not materialize, they were told in 1990 about a birthmother in western Canada who was planning to place her baby for adoption. They heard about her from a physician's office they had contacted through Sonja's sister. Seven days after the young woman gave birth to a baby girl, she expressed her wish to place her child with Sonja and Seaton. They flew out west with their social worker to meet Nicole.

Sonja: "When we left Toronto, it was not yet definite. Every effort was made to safeguard the birth family's rights. We met the baby's birthparents and also some of their extended family members at the office of Nicole's social worker. During this time, we talked about many things, including the exchange of letters and photos. We were given gifts for the baby, including a quilt made by the great-grandmother. With the support of their family, the birthparents reconfirmed their decision to place their baby girl with us."

Seaton: "When it came time to leave the hospital Nicole literally handed Avalon to me. We were standing in a circle, and this beautiful baby was being passed around the circle to be held by everyone. The entire ward was crying. It was incredibly emotional."

Photo by Daniel St. Louis.

Lian, Sonja,
Avalon, and
Seaton.

When the couple returned to Toronto, Sonja had six more weeks remaining on an acting contract, and Seaton was fully engaged in his work as well.

Seaton: "Having a newborn baby was a huge adjustment. One day you have no children, and the next your world turns upside down. We were like a tag team because we wanted to look after Avalon ourselves, with no help. It was insane, but wonderful."

When Avalon was three, Sonja and Seaton started thinking about adopting a second child.

Sonja: "We briefly considered domestic adoption, but in the short time frame since Avalon's birth, circumstances had changed. We were older, and because we already had one child, we were given the impression that our chances of being chosen by a birthmother were less now. We looked into international adoption and soon learned that China seemed to be the most straightforward country choice."

After updating their home study and completing the extensive paperwork, including bank records, physicals, and fingerprinting for Interpol, their file was submitted in the fall of 1993. Eight months later they were given their referral.

Sonja: "Seaton was out of town, so I drove to the social worker's office preparing myself for another daughter and a baby sister for Avalon. Upon my arrival, and to my utter amazement, she said, 'It's a bit unusual, but it appears to be a boy!' I said, 'A boy? How can it be a boy? Are you sure it's not a mistake?' Seaton and I, although unprepared, were delighted."

But it was no mistake, and in June 1995, Sonja and Seaton travelled to China with a group of thirteen other couples to adopt seven-month-old Lian. At the time, out of several thousand babies adopted from China, Lian was probably the third boy to have ever been adopted in Canada.

Sonja: "It was a seamless process. Everything was so well organized and laid out. We spent two weeks there with Lian completing the adoption process and, of course, sightseeing. We drew a lot of attention in public, even more so, I think, because of Lian being a boy. Avalon, having always wanted a brother, met us at the airport upon our return with other family members and a great big sign that said, 'Welcome Home, Lian.'"

I have an opportunity to ask Avalon and Lian about their adoptions. Avalon shares with me what it was like to meet her birth family when she was ten.

Avalon: "My birth family came to a big barbecue that my mom's sister held for us in her backyard, with grandparents, cousins, aunts, and uncles. I remember giving this lady a hug, not knowing she was Nicole, my birthmother. I had seen pictures of her, but being a hairdresser, she kept changing her hairstyle, so I didn't recognize her. She's married now and has two blond-haired, blue-eyed sons. [Avalon is clearly a brunette.] The next day, my mom and I went to the town where Nicole had grown up. It felt like I was visiting strangers in a way, kind of awkward and not really emotional. But they were all so nice and welcoming. We've kept in touch with letters, and they send gifts for birthdays and Christmas. Nicole sent me a ring for my sixteenth birthday that I wear all the time. She was given it by her father when she turned sixteen. "

Sonja: "Avalon's birthgrandparents have her framed picture on the wall in their home along with their other grandchildren. They are very loving and thoughtful people. I have always been very sensitive to her and the decision she made — what she gave up. Nicole gave a bunny to Avalon that I kept in her crib for a very long time and a shelf in her nursery with her birth family's gifts and mementoes." Sonja's eyes well as she thinks about her daughter's birthmother.

Avalon: "I grew up knowing I was adopted. I was always open about it and not embarrassed by it. To me it is normal. I remember my mom telling me that I wasn't born in her tummy or Daddy's tummy or Opa's tummy. It isn't and it shouldn't be a big deal."

Seaton: "When we were growing up, adoption was not something that people talked about much, but I think that is changing. Over the years, I have become sensitized to people's comments and questions, but I am still caught off guard at times. In Lian's case, his adoption is visibly more obvious, and one day in the grocery checkout the cashier looked at Lian and then me and asked, 'Is your wife Chinese?' to which I replied with a simple no. She looked at me dumbfounded. Other people have asked, 'How do you feel about them not being your real children?' and I say, 'What do you mean — real children?'"

In 2006, when Lian was eleven, he and his parents went to China to visit the place of his birth.

Photo by Daniel St. Louis.

Lian and Sonja share a laugh.

Lian: "Maybe my birthmother was underage and she left me wrapped in a blanket somewhere. Maybe she had another child and couldn't afford to keep me, so I was abandoned."

Sonja: "Remember, in China the laws are strict and a woman can sometimes get into trouble with the authorities, so she decides to do it in secret? She had no other choice but to do it that way, but she took you to an orphanage where you would be taken care of."

At the time Lian was adopted, it was not common to see boys adopted from China; but in 2007, out of two hundred placements by the adoption agency Children's Bridge, twelve of them were boys.

Conditions at the orphanage where Lian was living have changed dramatically in thirteen years. A beautiful park now stands in its place. The new orphanage is located elsewhere. There is a new highway and sports arena, all evidence of China's increasingly thriving economy.

Photo by Daniel St. Louis.

Lian: "When we were there, I met my orphanage brother, a boy who had lived at my orphanage all his life, since before I was born. He was about twenty-five years old."

Sonja clarifies that this boy was mentally handicapped and, having never been adopted, was a companion to the children in the orphanage.

Lian: "They took us out for lunch, where we had a banquet of Chinese food, an early birthday cake for me, and chicken feet. It was pretty cool."

Seaton: "The chicken feet tested our mettle."

Sonja: "I rose to the challenge and ate one chicken foot."

The orphanage director invited Lian to return when he's older and to bring his sister back with him. The graciousness and hospitality of their Chinese hosts was heartwarming.

Hobbs joins the family portrait.

Sonja Smits and Seaton McLean parent their children as parents of biological children do. Their values and beliefs have been strengthened by the adoption process, their lives enriched beyond measure. As our time together is winding down, the photo albums come out, the memories are recounted, and the laughter resumes. The normal flow of the family begins again, just where it was before I interrupted their day.

151

Photo by Anne Kmetyko.

The greatest experience, the one that shakes a soul with hopes and fears,
the results of which are never-ending, and, incidentally, the one which pays
the biggest dividends, is to be found in the adoption of children.

Anonymous

To Russia With Love

The Smith/Sullivan and Havel/Anderson Families Montreal, Quebec

"If they had gone anywhere else, we would never know that we had a brother and sister."
— Elena Sullivan, daughter of Carol Sullivan and Gary Smith

WHEN MY HIGH school friend Carol Sullivan and her husband, Gary Smith, told me they were adopting two children from Russia in 1993, I must confess I was rather blasé about the news. In hindsight, my only excuse is that at around the same time I had given birth to our son; we were on concurrent journeys, but very different ones. After high school, Carol and I had gone in opposite directions: Carol had gone to Montreal and I had remained in Toronto.

Carol and Gary struggled for six years to have children biologically, before spending four years trying to adopt. In Quebec, the challenges of adopting children through social services are greater than in other provinces; after considering their options, the couple decided they were not prepared to wait a potential seven years to adopt domestically.

In another part of Montreal, Geoff Anderson and Alice Havel had arrived at a similar conclusion in their hopes of having a family. Unexpectedly, the paths of the two couples were about to converge in a way that could only be described as serendipitous.

In the early 1990s, international adoptions took place primarily from China and Russia. Both couples decided on Russia, because it seemed to be a smooth process and because they felt the integration of Russian children into a francophone environment might be less difficult. There were only two agencies working out of Russia in Montreal, and both couples chose the most expeditious one. They also dealt with the same agency facilitator, who undoubtedly played a very important part in the outcome of this story. Gary and Carol recall the early days of the process.

Gary: "We had been presented with three other situations before we received the dossiers of a sibling group of four: two girls, two boys. We had photographs and video of the children to look at, and it became such a dilemma. We felt that adopting all of them was not an option for us. What were we to do? We thought it would be wonderful to have the four children at very best close to each other."

Carol: "We decided we would apply for the two older children — Alexei, who was six, and five-year-old Elena. We were so concerned about what would happen to the younger children and asked the agency worker if there would be an effort to place them with a family in the same vicinity as us. They answered, 'We have to go to the next people on the list, and we can't make that guarantee.'"

This is the point in the story where the two couples' link to Russia, their adoption facilitator, Victor, decided to give fate a hand. Geoff and Alice had been presented with the dossiers of the youngest children — Anastasia, who was three, and Genya, two. Geoff called Alice at work and asked, "Are you ready to travel? We're going to Russia."

Alice: "We were concerned about Anastasia because we were told she was not talking. I decided to speak to a pediatrician to see what he knew about Russian adoptions. We weren't opposed to children with learning challenges, as I work in the education field, but I wanted to be prepared. We called the agency again; when asked about Anastasia's speech they said, 'Yes, she does speak — but only when she wants to.' It was then we also learned that another couple had expressed their desire to adopt the two older children, and the agency asked us, 'Would you like to meet the other couple?'"

When Geoff and Alice made the decision to adopt Anastasia and Genya, they called Carol and Gary to invite them for dinner. It was November 1994: the beginning of what would be a lifelong connection because of four beautiful children from Russia.

Carol: "We spent the evening trying to get to know each other and discovered we had several things in common. Gary and I also work in education — educators for the deaf, actually — and we also perceived Geoff and Ali as being socio-economically similar to us. We were just so relieved that they were an Anglophone couple in Montreal. We got along very well, and by the evening's end I think we all thought it could work well. Maybe it was divine intervention at work."

For the next three weeks, the couples communicated by phone as they prepared to leave on their Russian adventure. The next time they met was December 16 as they waited in great anticipation to board a nine-hour flight to Moscow.

Carol: "There were four other couples besides ourselves going over to adopt, who were going elsewhere once there. Because of the season, the flight was full of people with boxes of gifts for family members. And there we were going halfway around the world to meet ours! Once we arrived, we were whisked through customs and immigration and then quickly driven to catch the trans-Siberian train that would take us to our destination. The children were at an orphanage in Pervouralsk, thirty kilometres west of the Siberian border."

This is the part of the story where I feel as though I have stepped into a movie. The couples recount the memories of the twenty-nine hours they spent on this train together, in a strange land to meet their children. They had only blind faith in the agency in Montreal who had made the arrangements and a chaperone named Madame Dali guiding their journey.

Carol: "The four of us had a compartment with two bunk beds on each side and little space in between — so there we were for twenty-nine hours."

Geoff: "It was interesting to see the countryside and go by all the tiny snow-covered towns. There were no roads plowed anywhere. All the cars were parked in the garages and closed off. The only indication of life we saw was the clustering of people around the train stations."

Gary: "The Russian people wanted to practise their English with us. They treated us like we were stars. We were from Montreal, and they knew about the Montreal Canadiens (go, go, go). They gave us champagne and chocolate."

Carol: "We took turns going to the dining car — Geoff and I, and Ali and Gary — because it was so uncomfortable and also because there was a level of concern about safety.

We ate soup all the time and drank tea at night. It was very dry on the train. I lost ten pounds on the trip."

Alice: "We didn't have much advice on what to bring with regards to food, but I had packed some peanut butter and also Tang, which we mixed with our bottled water. Geoff was quite sick with a fever and cold, so we were taking care to keep him as hydrated as possible."

Carol: "It felt like espionage at times — there was an intrigue about not knowing what was going to happen next. When we were asked why we were in Russia, we would say, 'Visiting family' — we didn't know what the general population thought about adoption of their children."

The foursome reached Pervouralsk, and each couple was billeted with a family while there. Geoff and Alice were with an English-speaking family without a car, Carol and Gary with a non-English-speaking family who did have a car (and were therefore considered well-off).

Gary: "The city was very industrial, with rows and rows of identical apartment complexes. We were staying in different buildings that were close to each other, but the buildings weren't numbered and we were afraid if we tried to walk to each other we'd get lost. We weren't sure what the plan was except that we'd get into a car and be driven somewhere."

The following day, when their car approached the orphanage, a group of little faces pressed up against the glass windows looking to see who was arriving. Carol saw Anastasia and Genya first.

Carol: "There are your two — there they are! [I said.] We were quite taken aback when the orphanage director ushered us into the office and offered a suggestion — that we each take a younger and older child. In other words, change the original plan of which children we would adopt."

Gary: "Of course, that was out of the question. We had already started our bonding process through the picture we had of Alexei and Elena. Once you see a picture of them — that's it, they are your kids."

Geoff: "We were taken to a big room with beautiful wood floors, a piano, and toys at one end. Our first meeting was in that room. The children were there, accompanied by an orphanage worker."

Photo by Anne Kmetyko.

(from left) Genya, Anastasia, Elena, and Alexei prepare to leave Russia in 1994.

Carol: "I was a little uncomfortable with the way we were introduced to the children as their 'mama and papa.' Alexei, who was six, and Elena, five, had been with their birthmother for the first four and three years of their lives. They knew what their mama looked like, and I was not it! The worker with us was a godsend in helping us relate to the kids. We played with them for almost two hours, and they seemed happy having us just paying attention to them. It was fun, but surreal in many ways."

The following day Geoff and Gary drove together to Yekaterinburg, the regional capital, to take care of all the paperwork, while Carol and Alice went back to the orphanage to visit the children and bring them clothes.

Gary: "It was a wild ride. I was driving on a snow covered highway in a Lada, with Geoff crouched in the back. We couldn't see the road for the entire one-hundred-kilometre trip. I kept thinking about the potential of Carol widowed with two Russian children."

During the signing of the documents, the only sign of the paperwork's authenticity was their recognition of their children's names. For all they knew, they could have been buying a farm! After touring the city, including seeing where the Czar and his family had been assassinated, Geoff and Gary drove back to Pervouralsk.

The next day, the couples went to the orphanage to prepare the children for leaving.

Carol: "I'm not sure at what point the children were told what was happening. They knew they were going to live somewhere else, and with us, but they had lots of questions about what their life was going to be like. I don't think they realized the enormity of the change in their lives until the plane ride."

Gary: "All the kids in the orphanage there were around us as we were leaving. We were asked if we knew of any other couples who would adopt from their orphanage. At that point the kids wanted to get going. There was no sharing us. Alexei was the little leader, [he] picked up some bags and said, 'Okay, Papa, let's go!' He had no idea where he was going."

Geoff: "On the way to the airport Genya just howled, and that got Nastya started. It was hard for us to imagine what was going through their little heads. It was still dark then — we were taken on a little bus out to the plane for Moscow; so here we were on a tarmac with four little kids waiting for the doors to open."

As the two couples are telling me about all of this, I am thinking about my own family on vacations together, and how stressful it can be. The visual I conjure up in my mind is of the part in the movie when someone (besides the children) should be crying. When they finally arrived in Moscow, they learned that some of the luggage didn't arrive with them.

The new families were driven to the old Olympic Village complex, where they were given accommodation in one room each, with one bed, for the next two nights.

Alice: "All of a sudden we were parents and responsible for these little kids. It was overwhelming. I think our experiences getting out of Russia helped to develop a little trust in us on the children's part. By the time we were ready to leave, we were sharing comfortable laughter with each other."

Just as everyone thought they might get back home for Christmas, they found out that their flight going home was overbooked. There were only four available seats remaining. Geoff and Alice left with their children first, on December 24. Carol and Gary would be spending Christmas in Moscow, with plans to leave for home on December 27.

Carol: "I just cried and cried — I wanted to go home. We had no money and had to rely on our chaperone to take us out for meals. We played endless games of Uno and luckily were given the opportunity to call family at home as much as we wanted to, which was a help."

Gary: "On Christmas day we were given permission to go to a movie and a traditional Christmas dinner at the Moscow Sports Bar, a restaurant frequented by Americans. We also had a tour of the city and the open-air market. The kids were real troopers, but we were all anxious to get home to start our lives together. The trip home was a relief."

Photo by Anne Kmetyko.

Genja, Anastasia,
Elena, and Alexei
— still together.
Montreal 2008.

At this point in our discussion, the children join us to share some of their recollections of adjusting to life in Canada.

Carol: "Shortly after we came home, we all came together for a meal before New Year's and talked about how we would manage the transition as separate families and at the same time develop the kids' relationships. They had spent very little time together in the orphanage and needed our help in getting to know each other."

Both families had very little knowledge about the daily patterns of the children's lives, and it was a learning experience for them all. Because Gary and Carol are fluent in signing from their careers working with the deaf, this became a way they could communicate with their children in the early days. Geoff and Alice developed other strategies.

Geoff: "I remember the first night we were home, at bedtime, we took them to the bedroom they would share and tucked them in with some little hugs and turned the light out. Of course the crying started, and it got louder and louder. *What do we do now*, we thought! Ali and I went in and sat between the beds, and we each held a hand and stayed. That became our ritual every night — we'd sit and talk and hold hands for five to ten minutes, and they would nod off. We also discovered that they were used to being given permission to get out of bed in the morning, so we would have to go into their room and do that too."

Generally, the children adjusted well in terms of eating and sleeping. It was the educational and social aspects of life in Canada that provided the most challenges. Alexei went to kindergarten knowing no English; Elena was at home with Carol for more than a year before she entered school. In the beginning there were so many new and overwhelming experiences: haircuts, dental appointments, trips to the mall, different foods, and just life routines in general. Now nineteen, the eldest child, Alexei, shares his thoughts with me.

Alexei: "I still have strong memories of my home in Russia because I was with my birthmother until I was four," he says. "I remember the day they took Nastya and Genya and then me and Elena; I didn't know what was going on. We went to an older orphanage for a year, and then to a newer one. They separated us by age, so the younger ones were on a different floor. Everything was very organized: routines of meals, playtime, and sleep. They were kind to us."

Elena (age eighteen): "I remember a lot, but I don't have a mental picture of my birthmother. I know she's blond and kind of short. I would like to go back and see where we came from."

Alexei: "I remember thinking, *I'm on a new journey now, in new territory*. Everything was totally different — house, school, food, a scary basement. I think it took about two years to get used to it. English replaced my Russian — it was difficult."

Carol: "I think it was at least two weeks after we got home before we heard them laugh a spontaneous natural laugh — music to our ears. Holidays were such a wonder for them. We started celebrating each one as they came, and Elena couldn't get over the fact that she would have a birthday every year. 'Again?' she'd say. 'Again?'"

Photo by Anne Kmetyko.

Laughter abounds. (clockwise from bottom) Elena, Anastasia, Genya, Alexei, Carol, Gary, Ali, and Geoff.

Elena: "It was no surprise to us to know that we were adopted — I knew all along. Sometimes when I say to friends that I'm from Russia, I end up talking about my adoption. It's really no big deal, I know other kids who are adopted too."

The memories for sixteen-year-old Anastasia and fifteen-year-old Genya are far more remote, but they share their siblings' interest in going back to Russia to see their first home. I can see closeness they share … there's a lot of joking and laughter going on, and mutual affection. Genya, Anastasia, and Elena are particularly close.

Elena: "It is very good to know that there are at least two other people on this earth that we are related to. If they had gone anywhere else, we would never know that we had a brother and sister."

My impression of this adoption story is that it is like a marriage. It is now thirteen years into it, and the honeymoon is definitely over. The parents have helped one another navigate through all the growing pains together. It will be interesting when potential suitors and girlfriends arrive on the scene, only to be scrutinized by four parents instead of two! Most importantly, the children have found their places in each family's individual dynamic, while still becoming close as siblings through the occasions they can share as one very large family. I think that, in itself, is a reason for celebration.

Photo by Daniel St. Louis.

Making the decision to have a child is momentous.
It is to decide forever to have your heart go walking around outside your body.
Elizabeth Stone

Hand in Hand
The Gerrits Family
Chance Harbour, New Brunswick

"Well, why don't you adopt a kid like me?"
— Michelle Gerrits, daughter of Mike and Jenn Gerrits

THE FIRST TIME I heard the name Chance Harbour, New Brunswick, I felt that it was the perfect place for a family formed by adoption to live. Certainly chance can play a part in most adoption stories, but for Jenn and Mike Gerrits it took considerably more to make their dream of having a family become a reality.

Chance Harbour lies about half an hour west of Saint John along the south shore of New Brunswick. I have driven from Halifax, and the day is ending, the sunshine waning, as I arrive at the Gerritses' picturesque century home. The house's exterior is a warm shade of yellow, the wash is on the line, and their friendly German shepherd, Katie, greets me with some uncertainty. Jenn and Mike welcome me into their kitchen, fragrant with a roast turkey dinner. I am introduced to their children: Michelle, thirteen, Matthew, seven, and little Willem, three. It is suppertime at the Gerrits house, and they invite me to join them around a small round table to enjoy the delicious dinner. I am hard pressed to remember ever receiving a warmer welcome. It is close quarters around the table, so we get to know each other quickly as we chat about their family activities. Towards dinner's end, Willem has migrated onto my lap, quite fascinated by my reading glasses and anxious to help me eat my dinner. He is utterly captivating and is curious about my arrival. Matthew is quietly observing the goings-on, and I can see that he is paying close attention. Less than an hour into my visit I am feeling like part of the family.

Jenn and Mike struggled with infertility issues for more than four years before they realized that their dream was to have children, no matter how they came to them. Through their church pastor, the Gerritses became aware of a girl named Michelle in foster care who needed an adoptive family. Although the little girl had been placed in Saskatchewan, the placement had broken down and she was coming back to Chance Harbour.

Jenn: "Something grabbed my heart when we were asked to pray for Michelle, and as soon as we got home, I called her foster mother and social worker to inquire and express our interest. Even though we had originally applied for an infant, we decided in January 2002 to change our request to a sibling group. We completed the PRIDE course [Parenting Resources for Information, Development, and Education: mandatory adoption preparation] and began our home study. Before this was even completed we began having day visits with Michelle and were even able to take her on a holiday in PEI with us in August. The first night of the trip she asked us, 'Why don't you guys have any kids?' I answered, 'Maybe God doesn't think we're ready to be parents yet.' She said, 'Well, why don't you adopt a kid like me?' That night, I called her foster mother and said, 'It's time to get going.'"

When the Gerritses returned from holiday with Michelle, their home study had been approved, but her social worker was away. Upon her return, the social workers went on strike, and they were forced to wait again.

Jenn: "It was the longest six weeks of my life, but finally, in the first week of October, Michelle was asked by her social worker what kind of parents she would hope for. Her answer was 'I would want parents like Mike and Jenn.'"

The next day the phone rang, and Jenn heard the words she had been longing for: Michelle said, "Hi, Mom."

Mike: "It was like going to the hospital and having a baby."

In actual fact, the couple had begun the process nine months prior to the adoption of their first child!

It wasn't long before Mike and Jenn thought about adopting again, specifically a little boy named Matthew who had been in the same foster home as Michelle. While at church, Jenn thought she heard that there were some potential adoptive parents applying for Matthew. Jenn wasted no time in emailing the head of Community and Family Services in Saint John.

Jenn: "We wanted to make sure that he knew that we were hopeful that Michelle and Matthew, who had become very close in foster care, would be able to stay together. We expressed our desire to adopt Matthew. It became clear that Michelle was hoping for this too. We had a calendar that we marked up with pictures, and Michelle drew a picture of herself on the calendar with a bubble over her head. Inside the bubble was a sketch of a little blond-haired boy. She wanted to be a big sister very much!"

Mike: "When you're a kid in foster care, you learn quickly that kids don't usually go together if they are not biological siblings. Kids come and go — separately."

Jenn was as relentless as she had been with Michelle's adoption in making every effort to keep the process moving. Mike was busy with work, but he always supported her in their mutual goals. And Michelle was very good at keeping things moving too.

Jenn: "Infertility is extremely difficult to go through, but once you are able to move on from it and embrace adoption it can be so empowering. I felt that it was my fault that we weren't having a baby, and therefore my job to take the lead in our adoption plans. It's a little crazy how it takes over; you become a mother bear and just never give up!"

Mike and Jenn met with social services to present their case for adopting Matthew, and it was a very emotional discussion. Michelle had brought her drawing from the calendar that illustrated her dream of having a brother. She wanted them to know that Matthew had become just like a brother to her while they were together in care. The Gerritses waited five agonizing days for the decision before finding out that yes, they could adopt Matthew!

As difficult as it was, they did not share the news with Michelle until the adoption was more certain.

Jenn: "We told Michelle that she was finally going to have her wish of being a big sister, and when it registered with her that we meant a child and not her cats, Olivia and Timmy, she said, 'Oh, it's Matthew, right?' It was a very natural thing for her — it made sense in her mind because he already felt like a brother to her."

The family settled into life as a foursome and waited the requisite twelve-month period after Matthew's adoption finalization in January 2004 to apply for a third adoption.

Jenn: "Matthew would be turning four and Michelle ten, so we thought we'd consider a child of six or so. Just two weeks later, Michelle's social worker made an unofficial call

Photo by Daniel St. Louis.

Mike, Willem, Michelle, Jenn, and Matthew at a favourite beach near home.

asking, 'Are you settled on an older child, or what about a baby? Michelle's birthmother is due to deliver a boy soon, and would you be interested?' After I picked my jaw up from the desktop, I called Mike to ask the question and he said, 'Well, yeah!'"

The baby would be a full sibling to Michelle, and how thrilled she would be to be a big sister again! By this time, Mike and Jenn had become a very familiar family to social services. They were the topic of a number of meetings to discuss the potential placement; meanwhile, baby Willem was placed in foster care.

Jenn: "We didn't want Willem to stay in care for long, so I asked if we could foster him during the legal goings-on. Our worker didn't see why not, so once again we took on all the paperwork and a fostering home study. He was brought to us when he was three and a half months old. His foster mother didn't know about what had been happening behind the scenes, but in the two weeks leading to the placement she provided us with photographs of him. We sat looking at his pictures, finding it hard to believe he was going to be our son."

Mike: "We told the kids that we were going to be fostering for a while, which was fine for them; it was certainly something they understood. Until the guardianship order was

Photo by Daniel St. Louis.

Michelle and
Willem.

granted, Willem was going with a so-cial worker for supervised visits with his birthparents at least twice a week; all the while, Michelle [was] not aware they were her birthparents too."

Jenn: "The visits were somewhat disruptive to Willem's routine, but I have to say that they didn't miss one visit. Their birthmother is not capable of taking care of them, but she loves those kids. She has their pictures all over her walls."

On a family camping trip in July, Jenn "happened" to call their social worker on her cellphone while an unsuspecting Mike was in Canadian Tire (their second favourite store after Tim Hortons).

Jenn: "I just wanted to check up on things and find out what was hap-pening with the guardianship order!"

The birthparents agreed to relinquish Willem as long as visits could continue up until fi-nalization, which would afford them a thirty-day period to change their decision. The waiting was again torture. Towards the end of the thirty days, Mike was with the children when he saw one of the adoption officials who was familiar with their case. He started congratulating them about Willem. This hastened Mike and Jenn's decision to tell Michelle that Willem was her full biological brother.

Jenn: "We asked our social worker to be present, in the event that we needed her sup-port. I remember her saying to Michelle, 'The baby is your full sibling — your biological

Photo by Daniel St. Louis.

brother. Willem's birthparents are yours too.' Michelle was uncharacteristically speechless, and a little teary — but okay. She is all about family: the more the better. There's never been any indication of any kind of favouritism towards Willem. She simply loves being a big sister to both of the boys, biological or not."

I asked the Gerritses what it has been like adopting older children and now Willem as a baby.

Jenn: "When you take the PRIDE training, they try to prepare you for the extra challenges you might face adopting older children. You almost think they might break all your dishes and burn your house down. I suppose there are extreme cases, but for us not so far. Michelle 'honeymooned' for almost three months because she just wanted to please us. When she started to argue and give us a hard time, we were so relieved because it meant she was testing us to see what we would do. Sometimes in the heat of thing she'd say, 'I want to go back to my birthmom,' and we would tell her, 'It doesn't matter what you do, you are stuck with us — we love you and this is your family forever.' We also think that Willem coming has confirmed some things in her mind — that while her birthparents love her and Willem, they are not able to be parents to them."

Family portrait.

It is a big concept for a little girl. Michelle has been with the Gerritses for six years now, and turned thirteen in March of this year. She celebrated with four of her friends and her mom on a chauffeur-driven shopping trip. I am certain that Mike and Jenn have many more family adventures planned for their three children in the years ahead. There will be milestones, special occasions, and adventures on the beautiful beaches surrounding

Chance Harbour — a place where fate and a mother's perseverance went hand in hand to form a family.

Update: Since this writing in the fall of 2007, Michelle and Willem have enjoyed a visit with their birthmother, and Matthew has met his birthmother as well. Matthew has also learned he has two birthsisters! Mike and Jenn say this all seems right, because they want their children to know where they came from, and have the benefits of knowing their birthfamilies.

Photo by Daniel St. Louis.

Pretty much all the honest truth telling there is in the world is done by children.

Anonymous

And Baby Makes Three
The Drouin/Bolton Family
Halifax, Nova Scotia

"I growed in her belly and she borned me."
— Liam Drouin, son of Andrea and Hilary

IT IS RAINING steadily in Halifax, Nova Scotia: one of those October days that make you want to curl up in front of a fire with a book and a cup of tea. The tea is on as I meet Andrea Drouin and Hilary Bolton in their cozy home. Their son, Liam, is still at school. Andrea's mother, Linda, from Guelph, Ontario, is also there, visiting the couple and her grandson.

We get comfortable around the kitchen table and begin our discussion about two adoptions — Andrea's and Liam's — that illustrate distinct contrasts in time and circumstance.

Linda and her husband, Henry, had been married five years when they decided to pursue adoption. In Linda's first call to the Children's Aid Society, an appointment was made for the following week. They were interviewed separately and together, and a home study was conducted, both completed in a short time frame by today's standards.

Linda: "They asked us if we had a preference for a boy or a girl, and Henry left it up to me to answer. Because I have three brothers, I decided to tell them we wanted a girl. Only six months later, on October 6, 1970, CAS called to say that they had a six-week-old baby girl for us, and we brought Andrea home the very next day. We were thrilled."

There were quite a number of cousins in Andrea's family who were also adopted, and Linda talked to her daughter about adoption from a very young age.

Linda: "I was determined to be as open as I could be about Andrea's adoption. The sister of a friend of mine had only learned about her adoption in grade school, and she was devastated. I introduced Andrea to adoption with a storybook, and at the same time as reading it I would talk about her adoption."

Andrea: "When I was growing up, adoption was pretty much the norm with our own family, my six cousins, and others in school that were also adoptees. I don't remember ever not thinking or knowing that I was adopted. There were no teasing or negative comments surrounding my adoption."

Linda: "When Andy was three, I did become pregnant several times, but couldn't carry to term and as a result suffered more than three miscarriages. This was so traumatic, but I was very grateful to come home to Andrea. She was like a little mother hovering over me, offering to bring me water or other comforts. As much as we would have liked, we did not go on to having any more children."

Linda and Henry were given the standard information about Andrea's birthparents, like age, marital status, weight, height, hair colour, and occupations, but later learned that some of the information was inaccurate. Andrea would later search for her birthmother with Linda and Henry's full support and encouragement.

Andrea: "My birthmother was told that I was placed with a family in Nova Scotia, when in fact I was still in Guelph, where she lived. We also learned that while she claimed to CAS that she was a widow, in truth she had never married and also had a daughter seven years older than I, who[m] she was parenting. I had been the product of a forty-year affair."

Andrea started the search for her birthmother by placing newspaper ads and making phone calls in every Ontario town she went to, based on having one small clue to her identity. At birth she had been named Colleen and her last name was Wilson. Andrea was nineteen when the adoption disclosure registry was established, and she applied to it along with thousands of other adoptees and birthmothers. There was such a deluge of requests that it took more than ten years for her name to be entered, processed, and registered.

Andrea: "And that is how I found her. At first we communicated with letters through a social worker, but we eventually made direct contact. I was only to send letters to her work. My birthmother had not told one soul about me and to this day has not told my half-sister. She thought I might 'out' her to everyone and cause all kinds of disruptions to her life. Finally, when she trusted me enough to know I would not do that, we met in 2003. Having nine-month-old Liam with us distracted us from our mutual awkwardness. We have seen each other a few more times since then, and each time it is easier. Communication is not [easy], however, as she is living with her daughter and won't risk her finding out about me by mail or email. I can call their house, but if her daughter is there she will tell me I have the wrong number and hang up. I have a picture of them that I have displayed with our other family photos, and it's nice to at least have a face to see. I can only hope that my birthmom finds the strength and courage to someday tell her daughter about me."

Andrea's experiences as an adoptee, and ultimately in meeting her birthmother, undoubtedly influenced her approach and perspectives when faced with the unexpected opportunity to adopt a child with Hilary.

Andrea: "Hilary and I had been together about eight years when we took serious steps in 2001 to become parents."

They wondered if their same-sex status might delay an already long wait to adopt domestically, so they began trying to conceive using donor sperm. They had just started the process when a co-worker of Hilary's, who knew about their hopes to start a family, approached her with what would be a life-changing question. She asked, "Have you and Andy considered adoption? My sister is six months pregnant and thinking about options for her baby. Perhaps you would like to meet her?"

Hilary: "I went home to Andy as we both tried to digest this news, our heads spinning with questions. The following Saturday, we all met for dinner. We talked about things like our philosophies on parenting, our ideas of openness, and generally about our life. It went very well, but to this point we had not even discussed adoption. We were stunned when two hours later, my co-worker called to say her sister really liked us and wanted to go ahead with an adoption plan with us!"

Andrea: "At that point, things had to move very quickly, since we had not been approved to adopt. We knew our only two options were to contact the Children's Aid Society or Home of the Guardian Angel, the only private adoption agency in Halifax. They informed us that the first mother would be required to sign paperwork designating us as potential adoptive parents of her baby."

Andrea and Hilary were fortunate to find an independent social worker who was able to fast-track their home study. Their same-sex status was never an impediment. Religion, however, was another matter; although the first mother, who is Catholic, was not concerned, out of a personal bias her social worker felt Andy and Hilary would not be approved. A week before the birth of their baby, approval was granted, and they started painting and moving furniture. They were going to be parents!

Photo by Daniel St. Louis.

(from left) Hilary, Linda, Liam, and Andrea.

Liam Patrick Thomas was born by Caesarean section on July 11, 2002.

Andrea: "We jumped in a cab, and on the way to the hospital I told the driver, 'We need to get to Emerg — there's a baby being born!' to which he said, 'You don't look pregnant.' We were both present at Liam's birth and held him an hour later. His first mother chose not to hold him or see him. In Nova Scotia it is mandatory that all babies being placed for adoption must be either with the first mother during that time or in foster care. A foster family could not be found for him right away, so we were ecstatic to be able to stay in the hospital for four days and take care of him. It was wonderful."

I ask Andrea to share her most poignant memories of those early days.

175

Andrea: "I remember the nights with him walking the halls in the hospital. The night before he went into foster care, on one of our walks, I suddenly burst into tears. A nurse came running after me to see what was wrong. The emotional reality of it all had finally caught up with me. I was thinking, *Someone has given birth to this baby and we are going to parent him. What if she changes her mind?*"

Hilary, on the other hand, maintained a forced composure throughout.

Photo by Daniel St. Louis.

Liam knows how to charm the ladies in his life.

Hilary: "I knew he was going to be a boy, and I knew he was going to be ours."

After a visit with Hilary and Andrea, Liam's first mother left the hospital the day after Liam's delivery. This was her choice, and she also wanted the couple to make all the decisions related to Liam. She said, "You are his parents."

During the rest of the obligatory thirteen-day waiting period, Hilary and Andrea drove ninety minutes back and forth every day to spend an hour with Liam at his foster home. On the last day the tension of the situation peaked.

Hilary: "That morning, while we did last-minute diaper and formula shopping, Liam's first mother was at the agency signing the final documents. I think we were their first same-sex adoptive couple, and they had to re-type all the forms to reflect this. We were referred to as Parent I and Parent II, and with emotions so high we really had to focus on which one we were!"

Andrea: "Upon arriving at the agency I couldn't get out of the car with Liam's car seat. I simply couldn't fathom walking out of there with an empty car seat if she'd had a change of heart."

But Liam's first mother didn't change her mind, and he was officially their son.

Liam has been a joy in their lives.

Hilary: "He was such an easy baby to take care of — the first month he was barely awake!"

Friends and family are happy and supportive about their decision. Linda enjoyed a surprise "granny shower" given by ten of her close friends and their daughters, and she goes east to spend time with her grandson when possible. Liam is part of a very mixed community of families, both traditional and non-traditional, and he attends a school that values diversity and tolerance.

Photo by Daniel St. Louis.

Andrea feels disappointed that Liam's birthfather has not chosen to be involved in his life, although he has plenty of male influences and role models.

Andrea and Hilary are in touch with Liam's first mother through emails and phone calls, but so far she has not met Liam, who is now six years old.

Andrea: "Because I was brought up in a closed adoption I didn't want Liam to go through searching and not having those questions answered. He knows he is adopted, and when referring to his birthmom says, 'I growed in her belly and she borned me.'"

As he grows older, the bigger questions will come. He and his mother have something meaningful in common, and that, along with his parents' love and openness, will serve him very well for the future.

Photo by Daniel St. Louis.

What greater thing is there for human souls than the feel that they are joined for life
— to be with each other in silent, unspeakable memories?

George Eliot

The Next Chapter
The Park Family
New Minas, Nova Scotia

"Our hearts are very much in China."
— Sandra Park

MY FIRST INTRODUCTION to Arnold and Sandra Park was in my dentist's office, on the cover of a 2006 *Canadian Business* magazine. Arnold's successful career, most recently as the former CEO of McCain Foods Canada, was profiled, but the photograph clearly indicated that the article's content was about much more than business. The Parks were pictured with their three young daughters, whom they had adopted from China. I was immediately compelled to speak to this sixty-something couple to hear first-hand how they are managing the second chapter in their parenting. They are also parents to four adult children and grandparents to nine.

I meet with them and their youngest daughter, Lily, at their home in New Minas, Nova Scotia. The newly built home still needs some finishing touches, but it is nonetheless breathtaking. The location affords spectacular views of Minas Basin and the Bay of Fundy, which today is unfortunately shrouded by cloud and a fine misting of rain.

As we settle into the spacious and comfortable family room, four-year-old Lily makes certain that we don't forget about the real reason for my visit. She captures my heart with her mischievous brown eyes and engaging grin before her parents even speak.

Photo by Daniel St. Louis.

The Parks were not strangers to the idea of adoption when they began their journey in earnest. They had been foster parents and had talked about adopting all their married life. But Arnold's busy career, four children, and more than twenty moves left little time for anything else, until a chance meeting in late 1997 started the wheels in motion. They were attending a dinner in Ottawa honouring the visit of the prime minister of Japan, Ryutaro Hashimoto, to our nation's capital.

Sandra: "At the reception we met a woman who excitedly told us about the adoption of her little girl from China as a single mother. I remember saying, 'Oh, we'd be too old.' She asked if I would like her to send us information about the agency she had worked with, and I said, 'Okay.'"

Sandra and Arnold keep an eye on (from left) Lily, Sarah, and Molly.

The Parks learned about China's one child policy (traditionally and preferably boys), which became law in 1979 in order to prevent the swelling of the overpopulated country. In the early 1990s, the Chinese government allowed more foreign adoptions in an effort to find homes for the high numbers of abandoned baby girls who wound up in orphanages.

In less than a month, Sandra and Arnold decided to proceed, and they contacted Ottawa-based Children's Bridge to begin the process. The Parks' file was sent to China in June 1998, and the following May they became part of Group 59, on their way to meet fourteen-month-old Sarah, known from birth as Zhang Sanhua. She was born in Zhangjiagang city in Jiangsu province.

Sandra: "Each group had a volunteer leader, and we stepped up to volunteer for all three trips. The first time it was the blind leading the blind. The groups were also accompanied by Chinese guides, who were critical to the trip. They not only maintained the strict schedule we were following, they navigated us through the process physically and answered any of our questions or concerns. Children's Bridge had planned everything so well that the process was virtually flawless."

When it came time to meet Sarah for the first time they were directed to a large room where each baby was brought in, held by a nanny. Tears of joy flowed freely during the poignant introductions.

After all the paperwork was completed, the Parks spent another ten days sightseeing with their new daughter and the rest of the group of happy families.

Sandra: "It was just a wonderful trip. China is an absorbing culture, and it was fascinating and heartening to see the Chinese expressing their appreciation with thumbs up and smiling gestures to us. They very evidently wanted us to know their happiness about us adopting their country's children."

When Sarah came home she was welcomed with open arms by the whole Park clan. I

Photo by Daniel St. Louis.

can't help but think that at times the Park children must have wondered about their parents' decision to adopt at their stage in life.

Sandra: "Their concerns, other than the obvious ones, were more about our potential longevity and our ability to care for a young child until her independence. We have everything in place in the event that something happens to us before then, and one of our children has agreed to step in as legal guardian if the time comes."

Their experience of adopting Sarah was so positive that the Parks returned to China in January 2002 to adopt two-year-old Wu Fu An, now named Molly. She was born in the city of Wuhan in the province of Hubei. Molly had spent almost all of her life in the orphanage, and at their first meeting her demeanour was distressing to see.

Sandra: "When Molly was brought to us she was sleeping, but even in sleep she was clearly distraught; actually sobbing in her sleep. In the early days, her posture was hunched over, as though she was protecting herself. After coming home, she seemed to adapt well, but in hindsight there was more under the surface than we knew."

By the time Sandra and Arnold returned for their adoption of seventeen-month-old Lily, Chinese adoptions were probably peaking at about fourteen thousand children leaving China to go to homes in North America and Europe each year. It was June 2005, and at a hotel in Nanchang nicknamed "the Baby Hotel," it was a familiar sight to see international visitors proudly holding their new babies. At any given time, the hotel could accommodate two to three hundred couples in the process of adoption.

The Parks' youngest daughter, originally named Yu Ruo Xin, was born in Xinyu City, Jiangxi province, and had been found near the gates of a civic building. Lily had been in foster care up until her adoption.

Sandra: "Lily was very attached to her foster mother, and as with the other girls, we had only a few hours of transition time with the orphanage officials before we were on our own. The touring time was our chance to begin bonding. Also, we knew this would be our last adoption because of our ages. China was more flexible at the time regarding the age of the adoptive parents, but we were at the upper limits."

Recently, China has imposed much more strict requirements on potential adoptive parents, including lower age limits. This will result in a slowdown in Chinese adoptions and a possible increase in adoptions from other countries such as Ethiopia, Kazakhstan, or India.

The Parks' hearts remain passionately in China, and Arnold has poured his business experience into serving on the Board of Directors of Children's Bridge as well as becoming president of the Children's Bridge Foundation from 2003 to 2007. The foundation's purpose is to assist orphans in China who are unlikely candidates for adoption but whose needs are high. Thus far, the organization has raised upwards of $500,000 that has been directed towards educational aids, sports and music equipment, and even medical procedures where needed. The goal is to raise at least $250,000 annually to continue this valuable work.

Meanwhile, in this hilltop home in Nova Scotia, the daily pace is frenetic by any standards. Three energetic girls provide activity from six in the morning until ten at night. They live

Photo by Daniel St. Louis.

Arnold has his hands full …

very full lives here in Canada, but Sandra and Arnold honour their heritage by participating in Chinese celebrations and attending functions organized by Children's Bridge. When Lily is a little older, they will return to China with the girls and visit each one's birthplace.

Sandra: "We are very proud of our girls' ancestry, but will let them take the lead in terms of how much they want to become immersed in it. Already they are showing varying degrees of interest. We celebrate their personalities as individuals as well as the birthright that unites them."

During my time with the Parks, Arnold is relaxed and seems content to listen as Sandra and I chatter on. I realize that he is outnumbered by females this day, as in fact he is most days! He invites me to watch a video of their first trip to China to adopt Sarah, and it is during his accompanying commentary that I see the emotional magnitude of the girls' adoptions.

Arnold: "Our reactions were the same: very highly charged emotions. Adopting our girls has been three of the best decisions we have ever made."

For a man whose life has been composed of many significant decisions, both professionally and personally, that's saying a lot.

Photo by Daniel St. Louis.

People ask me, "What about gay adoptions? Interracial? Single Parent?"
I say, "Hey, fine, as long as it works for the child and the family is responsible."
My big stand is this: Every child deserves a home and love. Period.
Dave Thomas

Daddy and Papa
The Kaiser/Carter Family
Porters Lake, Nova Scotia

"The best part of being a parent is having your kids put their arms around you and hold on with everything they possess."
— Gary Kaiser, father of Wolfgang, Reichen, Michaela, and Sophie

FIRST, THE SOUND of toddler feet approaches at warp speed. Then the door to the immaculate downtown home swings opens, and I lower my gaze to a lopsided grin and the most enormous blue eyes ever: I am smitten. Two-and-a-half-year-old Reichen, safely holding his daddy's hand, welcomes me and leads me to meet his older brother, Wolfgang, and his baby sister, Michaela.

The evidence of children is everywhere — an array of photographs, pint-sized shoes neatly lined up at the door, scattered books and toys, and diapers tucked away in what used to be an entertainment centre. It is a typical family home, with one exception: in this family, there are two fathers, one Daddy, the other Papa. Quickly I come to realize that in this case, the term "exception to the rule" is a very good thing.

Darrin Carter and Gary Kaiser met when they were both in their early twenties. Neither had ever thought seriously about becoming a parent until they had been together for almost ten years. It was then the mid-1990s, and same-sex adoption was not yet legal in Canada. Gary's sister was about to have a baby. As they watched her nearing her due date, a seed was planted in their minds.

They moved to Toronto in 1998 and attended a meeting at the 519 Centre one evening. The topic of discussion was adoption. Two of the options presented were surrogacy and co-parenting, where a gay and lesbian couple shares the custody of biological children. The seed continued to germinate.

Gary: "We don't feel that biology necessarily makes a parent. We wanted to be parents 100 percent of the time and to be consistent throughout our children's development. As we weighed all possibilities, adoption became more evident as the means to achieve our goal to have a family. We considered private adoption, but the law allows the birthmother a period of time in which to change her decision. We dreaded that possibility, particularly if we were to become emotionally invested.

"Finally, because we were open to adopting older children, we decided to pour our energy into adopting through the public system. Our first calls were to the Toronto Catholic CAS [Children's Aid Society]. Well, I think we gave about eight of their staff coronaries when we mentioned we were a same-sex couple! So we quickly moved on to Toronto CAS, and there we were welcomed with open arms."

Darrin: "After the initial intake meeting, the requisite parenting courses, and an exhaustive home study, we proceeded to hound our social worker regularly. Finally, eighteen months into our journey, she told us about a ten-month-old boy, born at twenty-six weeks weighing in at less than two pounds. He had undoubtedly had a very poor start, exposed in the womb to drugs and alcohol, and was not expected to survive.

"His first seven weeks were spent in the NICU [Neonatal Intensive Care Unit], and he also made it through emergency hernia surgery. This little guy was clearly a fighter! In his ten months of foster care, it became apparent that Wolfgang would need parents who could keep up with his high-energy personality. Luckily, his foster mother felt confident that we were ready for the challenge.

"Wolfgang's homecoming was both exhilarating and terrifying. He suffered from night terrors and was developmentally delayed in several areas. He resisted affection at first, although gradually a trust developed to the point where today, at four and a half, he loves to snuggle and be close."

Gary: "When Wolfgang was eighteen months old we filed the necessary paperwork to apply to adopt another child. A month later, CAS contacted us, this time about Reichen. He, too, was believed to be delayed, and it was uncertain if he'd also been affected by drugs and alcohol as well. Without any hesitation, we said, 'Of course we'll take him!'

"Thankfully, six weeks later Reichen was assessed as perfectly normal, and a lineup of potential adoptive parents began to form. Ultimately, we were chosen because of our initial willingness to adopt him regardless of any potential problems. We brought one-year-old Reichen home on December 19, 2003. Christmas was spent nursing him through pneumonia, but we could not have been happier.

"Just as we were settling into a routine with the boys, and I was about to board a plane to Newfoundland, our social worker called yet again. 'Are you sitting down? Reichen's birthmother has had another baby! Are you interested?' Before the question was finished, I quickly answered, 'Oh God, yes! Bring him over!' Our original intent had been to adopt four boys, so I assumed this child was also male. I was incorrect. Nine-week-old Michaela changed the game plan. Now our fourth child will have to be another girl, to keep the teams even!"

So life for these five has settled into a remarkably smooth routine. Work schedules allow one of the dads to be with their children almost all the time. They enjoy a wide circle of close friends and extended family, all of whom wholeheartedly support their decision to adopt. It is evident that they are strongly committed to each other and to their children.

Gary: "Because we are a same-sex couple and therefore obvious, we will never have to worry about when to have the 'talk' about adoption. In fact, we talk about adoption almost on a daily basis. In finalizing Reichen and Michaela's adoptions, we've tried to talk about the process with the boys in ways they can understand. First and foremost, we never want any part of it to appear secretive to them, so that they might interpret it as something to be ashamed of. We make a big deal of all aspects of the adoption process and try to celebrate each successful step."

Darrin: "We encourage lots of communication about all subjects, including how to deal with any negativity the kids may face. One day, Wolfgang was watching a kids' television

Photo by Daniel St. Louis.

The family pooch joins in.

program and asked, 'Where's Mommy?' I explained to him that there are many different types of families, some with moms and dads, and others with only moms or only dads. I reassured him of our love for him and our family, and he happily went back to *Max and Ruby*."

Gary: "We can't predict when or how outside challenges will present themselves. While we have the support of the majority of the other parents at Wolfgang's school, something surprising happened when I picked him up one day. Each of his classmates came out of the classroom carefully carrying a small plant grown from seed with a card for Mom for Mother's Day. The teacher came over to me and quietly said, 'We didn't get him a card because he really doesn't have a mommy, does he?'

"I restrained myself from losing my cool and simply said, 'Well, he has grandmothers, and lots of aunts. He could have given any one of them the card, couldn't he? He could even have

Photo by Daniel St. Louis.

Reichen, Darrin, Sophie, Wolfgang, Michaela, and Gary.

given it to either his dad or me, and we would have loved it. I hope you didn't exclude him from the activity because of something as silly as that!'

"Her awkward response was, 'We really didn't know what to do.' As there are other same-sex parents in Wolfgang's school, and because it is becoming increasingly common, I thought that it couldn't have been the first time she'd crossed this bridge. Maybe no one said anything before."

Gary: "We share the same hopes and fears as all parents. We fear for their safety and health, and we worry about not being there for them or not being able to help them when they need us."

Darrin: "As they grow older and their worlds expand, they will start getting involved in various club activities and making new friends. Challenges may arise where they will have to deal with the adoption issue, like why they have two dads coming to their soccer games."

Gary: "Because we will always encourage open dialogue about anything and everything, we hope they will be secure enough to talk openly about their adoption and, if they choose, about our non-traditional family. We would never want them to feel like they don't belong, either to our family or to society. We strongly desire for them all to grow up proud of who they are, how they've been brought up, and to have a strong sense of self.

"The best part of being a parent is having your kids put their arms around you and hold on with everything they possess. To know that, right now, we are their whole world and that no matter what we look like in the morning, or how many times we say no, their love for us is never-ending. Our greatest joy is to see them cross some milestone and see the pride that they feel in that accomplishment."

I ask Gary and Darrin what their greatest hopes for their children are.

"Funny, this is a question that CAS asks all their potential adoptive parents. As it was in the beginning of all this, our answers are still the same: if our children grow up to be doctors, lawyers, entrepreneurs, ditch diggers, or coffee servers, it makes no difference to us. Our only hope is that they are able to support themselves and to be happy in what they are doing. We want to be able to leave this world knowing that they'll be okay."

There is absolutely no doubt in my mind that they will be.

Update: In September 2007, I visited Darrin and Gary in their spectacular home overlooking Porters Lake just east of Halifax, Nova Scotia. They have accomplished two more of their life goals: adopting their fourth child, Sophie, and leaving Toronto to establish their family in a part of Canada they love. When Michaela was eighteen months old, the couple updated their profile and again applied to adopt with Toronto CAS. After spending ten months in foster care, second daughter Sophie joined her sister and brothers to "even the teams" in September of 2006. Two-year-old Sophie, four-year-old Michaela, five-year-old Reichen, and seven-year-old Wolfgang are thriving and happy. It is wonderful to see all the progress the children are clearly making with their parents and siblings, but most importantly to experience the love this family shares. They are going to be more than fine.

The Professionals

Human progress is neither automatic nor inevitable. Every step towards the goal of justice requires sacrifice, suffering, and struggle; the tireless exertions and passionate concern of dedicated individuals.
Martin Luther King, Jr.

Sandra Scarth

Bachelor of Social Work

President, Adoption Council of Canada
Adoptive Mother

Photo by Chris Hardy.

THE ONLY WAY I can stop Sandra Scarth in her tracks to give me an hour of her time is to meet her at the Adoption Resource Exchange in Toronto before the fall meeting of the Adoption Council of Canada. She is an extremely busy woman, and, it seems, has been so all her life. She has been working in the field of adoption in Canada for fifty years, starting in rural Manitoba after getting her degree in social work in 1957.

"I was the worker for all provincial social services in a very poor area," Sandra says. "The city workers handled most of the baby placements, so I took on some of the more challenging ones, like older children and sibling groups. I was unmarried and very green about it all, but I had a very good supervisor who mentored me. After four years, I moved to Vancouver and worked at the Catholic Children's Aid and then to Toronto at the Toronto Children's Aid for fourteen years as an adoption worker and supervisor."

Sandra and her husband have four children, two of whom were adopted at ages five and nine from the child welfare system. I ask her if her professional experiences made the personal ones any easier. She answers, "I was just like everyone else — and along the way needed some support from other professionals; when the way we had parented our biological children wasn't entirely successful with our adopted children, we needed to know why. Our experience helped me understand the importance of preparation and post-adoption support. Jan Thompson, another social worker at the agency, and I developed a course called 'Living with Adoption' that was offered at York University in the early 1970s. We hoped for twenty participants and were astonished that more than double that number arrived at the first session. Shortly after that, we incorporated group preparation into our regular adoption home study process and set up the first post-adoption support groups within the agency to respond to the need."

In 1982, Sandra moved from the CAS to manage the adoption unit of the provincial government. "It was very bureaucratic, and I wanted it to be run for adoptive parents and children. I think I managed to get the staff to see it as a service to the public."

In 1986, Sandra took over the policy division, which was broader in its responsibilities; while there she worked on adoption legislation and tried to get open records through. In 1991, she became the founding executive director of the Child Welfare League of Canada and was there until 1997. Shortly after, Sandra was invited to sit on the Board of Directors of the Adoption Council of Canada; she became president in 2002, where she remains today.

In her career Sandra has seen many changes and much progress in adoption. "I think in terms of secrecy and openness, we've come a long way," she comments. "In 1968, the belief at the CAS of Toronto, the largest agency in the country, was that the birthparents should go away, forget about it, and trust the agency— and a few of us in the adoption department didn't like it even then. I didn't believe for one minute that they would go away and forget about it. Adoptive parents were given limited information about the children they were adopting, told they should accept the whole child and all the child brings — that's fine, but parents needed to know what that was. I had been used to much more freedom to provide information where I had worked, and spent a lot of time encouraging colleagues to open up and be more forthcoming about information. We were told there was a policy about not giving written information; however, I argued that the policy was not written anywhere, so with the reluctant agreement of one supervisor, some of us started giving full information to people anyway, in typed forms, and then didn't tell anyone else. Gradually, over the next few years, in the 1980s and '90s, the practice changed:

birthparents and adoptive parents started to speak up wanting more information. That was the driving force in opening up the system."

In 1979, the Adoption Disclosure Registry was established to assist adoptees and birthparents in registering their requests to reunite, if both parties wished to do so. With efforts since 1998 to introduce a bill that would make the process more expedient, the registry has been done away with; new legislation is currently being formulated for Ontario. (Adoption Disclosure Bill 12, which includes a contact veto, was passed in May 2008.)

"What the media misses when they talk about the issue is that this is about adult adoptees, not children. Children are protected up to a certain age. When birthmothers wish to keep anonymity, they can do so with a disclosure veto," Sandra says. "I always think about who the innocent party is in all of this, and it's the adoptee. They didn't ask to be put into this position; they didn't ask to be told they can only have half a history. I remember one woman in particular who said, 'I look in the mirror and end there.' None of the rest of us have to deal with that. My sympathies are with the adoptee. If the question of rights overlap, I always come down on the rights of the child over everybody else. But the issues of openness are complicated and emotional, and how adoptees, birthparents, and adoptive parents deal with it is not predictable. That's why I think having a reunion registry would help negotiate these issues so that there's not carte blanche, and everyone respects each other's boundaries.

"In our case we provided both our children with as much information as we could obtain and told them we would help them to find their birth families if they were interested. They responded very differently. We had little information about our son's history, and he had no memories of his family. He wanted to know more. He registered with the reunion registry, but he couldn't wait. We knew where he was born, so with the help of his brother-in-law, he took a day trip to that area and, through the local newspaper, found his birth notice and his father's death notice, which told him he had five older sisters we knew nothing about. Later that day, a waitress in a coffee shop told him she knew his cousin, and that evening he met three of his five sisters and heard about more relatives. That same weekend, we met his oldest sister, who had registered with the reunion registry and with whom he maintains an ongoing relationship. Although the relationship with the other sisters did not work out as well as he had hoped, the whole experience helped him to understand himself better and also strengthened our relationship.

"Contrary to our son's story, our daughter had visits with her parents until she was seven, and had some memories of that. She told me over several years that she was not ready to reconnect with her birthparents. She did become interested at age forty-three after having her second child. She felt empathy for her birthmother, realizing how terrible she would have felt if she had lost her children. She used the reunion registry and found this helpful. She had an initial visit and then took her children the next day to meet their birthgrandmother. She has found the experience quite emotional, in that she discovered that when she was taken into Children's Aid care, her birthmother was also forty-three. They are developing a relationship by phone and letter, and a second visit is planned."

Sandra's personal experiences have and will continue to offer more insight in the ongoing journey of adoption as both of her children move forward on theirs. As we continue our conversation, I ask Sandra about adoption legislation across Canada with respect to consistency from province to province. "It will likely never happen," she says. "I believe it should be more consistent, but all provinces would have to agree to changes, and that is not a high priority. Legislation, however, has improved in the last ten years. The good news is that efforts are now being made to provide more consistency in practice. A number of provinces have begun to require the use of the standardized SAFE adoption home study model and the PRIDE adoption education package. This will provide consistent and improved education and preparation of prospective adoptive parents.

"Another area that needs addressing is the placement of older children out of foster care. I think we've done a dreadful job compared to the United States, and that's because there's no federal involvement here. The U.S. provides incentives to each state to place more children and therefore receive more funding, has provided support to the Adopt U.S Kid website, and also gives money to national recruitment efforts. In Canada, the federal government plays a very minor role in domestic adoptions. The Adoption Council of Canada manages the only national recruitment effort through its websites, but it does not have the funding to provide the kind of regular public awareness campaign that is needed to find more families for the waiting children.

"The federal government claims to have no role in domestic adoption, since the provinces are responsible for social services; however, I believe the federal government should have a role supporting research and national data collection for data both on Canadian foster children and on those available for adoption. There is a precedent for the federal government to be involved in national data collection as Health Canada funds and manages the Canadian Incidence Study of Reported Child Abuse and Neglect. Every province and territory collects foster care and adoption data differently, and with the help of a federal/provincial working group it is collected and released every four or five years, with the caveat that the data cannot be compared province by province. That is not useful. By the time it is available, the numbers have changed. By comparison, in the U.S. data is collected every six months: when every child goes into care, when that child is referred for adoption, and when the child is placed. So there is a running record, and the states are able to assess the outcomes of their efforts. We absolutely need to be doing this in Canada."

I ask Sandra if she can tell me how many children are in foster care in Canada, and how many of those children are Crown wards available for adoption placement.

She answers, "No one knows." She estimates perhaps 85,000 children in care, with 25,000 of those available for adoption. "The number that are actually placed based on the last domestic adoption figures I saw is about eight hundred [3.2%]. In contrast to Canada's low rate of placement, Illinois reduced its foster care population by one half because of the incentives from the federal government. So we really have a problem in Canada. Certain provinces like New Brunswick and Alberta have taken the lead in recruiting adoptive families, and Ontario is making an effort now too. But adoption is underfunded, it's under the radar, foundations aren't interested, and there's virtually no policy work being done.

"Another factor that affects and slows the movement of children in foster care into permanent homes is the court system. Again, every province has varying legislation in terms of how long biological parents can maintain rights, and children go back and forth from foster to familial care. That's the first problem, and then, when they are freed for adoption, it can take up to six months or longer to go to court. Meanwhile, that child is waiting. That is a huge area that needs reform.

"Another interesting and positive development is guardianship rather than conventional adoption. Adoption isn't the be-all and end-all — it's one form of permanency. Guardianship might appeal to grandparents or kin looking after children, because it doesn't cut the family tie. It might also appeal to teens who still maintain ties to family. I believe it is much better than foster care, because it's an intention to permanency that you are there for the child for the rest of that child's life."

I ask Sandra about education and support in adoption, both before placement and after finalization.

"A lot of provinces have post-adoption services, but in some provinces they are quite minimal and again underfunded. They may not be adequate for foster parents who wish to adopt but who worry about the loss of the supports they need to help them raise the children. The other thing we need to work on is mental health services that are appropriate for adoptive families, that don't blame the parents for the challenges the children present but help them to understand and manage the issues better.

"In terms of education, currently adoption is not covered in any great detail as a part of any social work program that I know of. I think it would work well as part of an adult education curriculum in colleges. Right now the specialized adoption training available is only for people with a social work degree, and it's run in conjunction with the University of Toronto— so that is a missing piece."

Sandra could say much more on the topic that has been her life's work and passion. There are more people all across Canada who share her commitment and the common goal of keeping children's best interests at heart in the complex issues surrounding adoption. You will find them working in both rural areas and cities, with birthparents, adoptees, and potential adoptive parents. You will find them working very long hours for inadequate compensation. You will find them sharing tears, giving hugs, and holding the hands of children who want only what they deserve: a loving, stable family and a place they can call home. It is impossible for them to accomplish their goal without the focused attention of our governments, both provincial and federal. The most positive progress, such as openness in adoption, has come about because of the advocacy of individuals and groups of adoptive parents and adult adoptees. They are the ones at the grassroots level most affected by past adoption practices. It is a pity that we have not found better ways to give voices to the children who wait for permanent families. We really need to focus on that.

Lynn Fearn Stewart
Bachelor of Social Work

Social Worker and Birthparent Counsellor

Photo by Chris Hardy.

AS WITH THE other adoption professionals I have interviewed, Lynn Fearn Stewart fits me in on the fly, between appointments. Her priorities these days lie mostly with birth families: mothers, fathers, grandparents, and even extended birth family.

She began her career with the Children's Aid Society in 1976 in the protection unit; in 1981 she took time off to have three children. In 1986 she began working in the adoption unit of Peel Children's Aid Society in disclosure until 1991, and then obtained her Bachelor of Social Work degree in 1993. She was conducting home studies, training, and community outreach education and somehow managed to have child number four. She has been working privately in the adoption field with adoptive families for fourteen years, and in the last seven years she has focused her attention on birthparent and birth family counselling. When we talk, I can feel her passion for and belief in this essential work. It is the key to ensuring that appropriate support is available for birthparents who are faced with making one of the most difficult and important decisions of their lives.

"Although I have not personally experienced adoption in my family, I have great empathy for and sensitivity to the complex issues surrounding adoption," Lynn says. "When I am asked to counsel the birthparents during the process, my role is not to make an adoption happen. I'm there to make sure that the birthparents receive the support they need and deserve regarding the decisions they need to make with respect to themselves and their child. I don't have to live with the decision, they do. I've had many birthparents say to me, 'We're so relieved and thankful that you are not forcing adoption on us.' I am there to be their advocate in the system. My goal is to help birthparents to be aware of all their options and the implications that come with those options so that they can make a well thought-out decision, which will ultimately result in the best future for themselves and their baby. Because this child is unplanned it's a no-brainer for birthparents that adoptive parents are in a more stable position and are more prepared to parent a child, [that] if the birthmother is poor the adoptive parents can easily provide a better life for the child— not something I need to point out; that would just make the birthparents feel very guilty should they decide to parent their child."

Not that Lynn hasn't had her share of supporting potential adoptive parents. She recounts the memory of a 3:00 a.m. phone call from a couple who had brought a baby home they hoped to adopt whose birthmother decided to parent before the end of the revocation period. The adoptive parents had hoped to keep the baby overnight to say a proper goodbye in the morning; however, they found the experience much too painful and asked that she remove the child. "I went to their home, and the couple were in the baby's room holding on to each other, crying — they said, 'We can't take it anymore.' I hugged them both, acknowledged their pain, and then changed the baby's diaper, dressed the baby, and left. It was indescribably painful for them."

Lynn's work is clearly not a nine-to-five proposition. She is on call virtually 24-7, and as a result her children are well aware of what constitutes their mothers' work time. Lynn says, "They have the best birth control: me. They see through me the grief that's associated with unplanned pregnancies."

I ask Lynn about the grief, and how she deals with it on a daily basis. She says, "It is one of the biggest challenges of what I do. I deal with loss on some level every day —but I know I can't fall apart, because then I can't help my clients and I will have no energy left to advocate for them. There is so much sadness in infertility and adoption. If the losses of infertility aren't resolved, couples don't move on to adoption well.

"There need to be more trained professionals doing this work, as many people involved in adoption can go on to struggle with unresolved grief issues. There needs to be more funding directed towards post-adoption support for everyone who needs it, as well as counselling throughout this lifelong process [for] the birth families, adoptive families, and adoptees. It should be considered a medical need, because that's what it is."

I ask Lynn to share her thoughts about what other factors would help relieve the systemic challenges in the adoption field.

"First of all, kids need to have education about the consequences of having a child as a teenager … what the realities of that look like. Perhaps if we had teens who have experienced unplanned pregnancies speaking about the realities of either raising their children or placing them for adoption, it would help others to make informed choices. This would probably work best if added to, say, a family studies curriculum that would encourage interactive dialogue.

"We need more specialized social workers that are truly equipped to offer the right help to the families. There are not enough of us that have the expertise to help the families deal with the complexities of adoption.

"Unfortunately, in adoption, there is the perception of two camps: public and private adoption practitioners. Sometimes there is a misconception that there is a conflict with providing adoption services for a fee and that private workers are not accountable for ensuring a child's safety. As professionals, we should all be here for the same purpose, and that is to arrive at a parenting plan that's best for the child or children. When a child's safety is not a factor in an adoption plan, there's no one right way — what's right is what works for that family. There is no place for control by professionals during each unique circumstance of adoption. Whether private or public, it is our job to respect and honour a birth family's right to making the best choice for their child's future."

What about open adoption, I ask. Are more families expressing a desire for openness?

"More and more people are embracing open adoption; the question becomes what level of openness. Five years ago, open meant meeting in a neutral location once a year. Now birthmothers or birth families may have a more significant personal relationship with the adoptive parents, sharing time throughout the year, or even family vacations. It's important to have a very clear understanding of each other's expectations by communicating honestly and respectfully, and then following through. There are misconceptions about open adoption — I have not had any experience with birthmothers out there stalking their children. They make adoption plans for a reason, and that reason is the welfare of their children. Birth families are people this birth child can still love, and it is important that we as professionals help all members of the triad develop respect for each other's roles.

"I think that it's so valuable to develop and build relationships between birth and adoptive families where possible. It is vital that adoptive families realize how influential they can be in helping their children understand the importance of birth families in their lives. We do not need to have children with divided loyalties; it is not a difficulty for children to have many people in their lives that love them. As biological or adoptive families we have to understand that we do not own our children, but we are here to guide them on a journey."

Lynn Fearn Stewart is one of many social workers who work tirelessly days, nights, holidays, and weekends to support and guide individuals and families through some of the darkest moments of their lives. We just need a lot more like her.

Wilma Burke

Bachelor of Social Work

Supervisor, Toronto Children's Aid Society,
Adoption Unit

Photo by Chris Hardy.

I HAVE NOT been to a Children's Aid Society office until the day I meet Wilma Burke, supervisor of the Adoption Unit for the Toronto office. There is security in the waiting room, and doors are unlocked to let me into the interior offices for our meeting. I am here to find out about adoption within the public system. Wilma worked in child protection for seven years, was an adoption worker for five years, and became a supervisor for Toronto CAS in May 1998. Things in adoption have changed dramatically since then.

"When I started, there was only one team of people focusing on adoption, and now there are two," Wilma says. "The team I supervise has ten social workers who work on the front end of adoption. We work with families who apply to adopt. We're responsible for co-facilitating the PRIDE training with foster care and kinship, conducting home studies, placement, and supervising the child's adjustment for a minimum of six months probation period after a child is placed. We are also responsible for being involved in the permanency planning for children placed into foster care who cannot return to their family of origin and determin[ing] whether adoption may best meet a particular child's needs.

"The other team primarily focuses on post-adoption support and services. This has expanded in recent years because we are finding there is such a great need for it. Funding to support adoption subsidies is provided through each agency's funding envelope. There are fifty-three [Children's Aid] Societies, and each society sets their own guidelines for providing subsidy assistance and post-adoption support. In developing an adoption plan for a child, [we] determine whether support and services are required both now and in the future. These support services may include a child and youth worker to assist with behaviour management, access to agency training for resource parents, respite care services, post-adoption support groups, and financial assistance to implement actions if necessary.

"Children's Aid Society has had the reputation of being a closed system, as traditionally children in child protection are legally freed for adoption through an order of 'Crown wardship with no access,' and only after all efforts to keep children with their birth families where possible. Adoptions through consents were generally closed as well, in that there was little openness between the child and their birth family once placed for adoption. That is why private adoption agencies really grew, as they offered another way of doing adoptions with openness. In 2006, changes to the legislation allow[ed] for adoptive placements of Crown wards with a level of openness based on the child's needs. We are still developing how this will be integrated into our practice."

I ask Wilma about children in foster care, and how long they stay in care before a plan is set into motion for permanency.

"For children under six, the time frame is up to a year ... and over six up to two years. But it may be longer before the child is legally free for adoption. Exploring and assessing family plans, scheduling court dates, and the appeal process can slow the timelines down. Generally, once a child is legally free and the thirty-day appeal process has passed, the child can be placed with their adoptive family. The needs of the child and the availability of a family who can meet the child's needs would also factor into the timelines. In our office, we have two doors that people come in, one to adopt and one to foster children. Generally families who come in for an application to adopt want to provide permanency to a child and often do not want to deal with the emotional demands of providing temporary care to children, which is an expectation in foster care. Approximately one hundred children a year are adopted through our society.

"We are fortunate to have a Wendy's Wonderful Kids Recruiter funded by the Dave Thomas Foundation for Adoption, who is looking at the older Crown ward population to assess these children more closely, with a view to permanency/adoption. It can get difficult when we go to court for the children to be freed up, because there is a perception by many that we will not be able to find families for them. There's a myth in our society that when children reach a certain age [over five], they're too old to adopt."

I ask Wilma to share her perspectives on how our government could best support the efforts of child welfare and Children's Aid Societies.

"Right now, funding supports children placed in foster care. There should be more flexibility in funding for adoption. Supporting adoption is ultimately less costly than funding foster care. Agencies should also be more flexible in terms of cooperation and collaboration of work. For example, our system is set up so that home studies are completed for applicants who live in our jurisdiction. This would make sense if all children could be placed with local families. However, there may be a more suitable family who can meet the needs of the child who resides in a jurisdiction where the local Society does not have the staffing to complete many home studies. Ultimately, we should be joining forces to find the best outcome for the child, regardless of funding issues.

"We have made much progress, however. There's been a lot of advocacy work done beginning in 2001 by the Ontario Association of Children's Aid Societies and the Child Welfare Secretariat. Required changes were identified in funding, legal issues, standardized practices, and post-adoption support. This advocacy has worked, and we have received a lot of what we asked for. However, change takes time to implement and incorporate in our daily practices. We are finding ourselves in a period of assessment to determine exactly what our needs [are] going forward. We are still early in understanding the true impact of these changes. Other legislative changes, I think, have also impacted the face of adoption in Canada. The concept of kinship care [guardianship by family] is growing, private and international adoptions are decreasing, and we are actually seeing more families wanting to adopt than there are children [not including the older children in foster care]. There is also a need for more social workers who are skilled in the area of adoption and post-adoption to guide people successfully through the complexities of these issues. I really believe there has been progress by our government to understand the importance of funding child welfare — I just think it will take some re-jigging to include more support for adoption initiatives, but we're certainly on the right track."

Wilma Burke has to excuse herself, practically in mid-sentence, to go to her next appointment. This conversation has probably been the first in a while where she has taken the time to actually sit down and articulate the state of adoption as it relates to Toronto Children's Aid. She's been too busy doing her job to think about it. Thanks for doing what you do, Wilma.

Michael Blugerman

Approved Adoption Practitioner

Photo by Chris Hardy.

IN A SOMEWHAT female-dominated profession, it has been enlightening to speak with a man whose passion and life's work has been adoption. Just as most adoptions seem meant to be, I believe it is so with people who enter and remain in the profession. It is a profession with little glamour, fortune, or recognition, and yet it is one that can profoundly affect so many lives.

Michael Blugerman is a professional who has stayed this difficult course. He graduated in social work from Waterloo Lutheran University (now Wilfrid Laurier University) and worked as a clinical practitioner counselling families and couples, doing custody work assisting lawyers around divorce cases, and doing some training. In 1979, when it became legally mandatory in adoption to have a home study completed by an approved practitioner, Michael decided to apply for approval; he was number five on the list.

"I found the process quite fascinating, I think because of my clinical background with families," he recalls. "In those days there weren't the extravagant efforts made by potential adoptive parents that are evident today. People wanted to present themselves in the best possible light but didn't come in to intentionally influence you. The challenge for the professional was to identify what their strengths were, what their weaknesses were, and what kind of characters they really were. The other fascinating part is that there isn't one area of social work or psychology that adoption does not touch on. There are marital and couple issues, parenting issues, inter-generational issues, fertility, sexuality, cultural, and so on. It can be very complicated work. All of these areas affect thoughts and perceptions about adoption.

"Almost everyone who considers adoption has gone through fertility issues to varying degrees. Back then the medical technology was not there, so couples would move to adoption sooner. Now it is not uncommon to see couples who have spent five to ten years, and a lot of focused effort and money, towards the goal of parenting. They try to put the grief and frustration aside and focus on the end goal, thinking, 'Adopt a child and we'll talk about the long-term ramifications later.'

"We are there for a small slice of time in these people's lives to help them become parents, but in that scenario it becomes a thought-provoking question: 'What is this picture going to look like in five, ten, or fifteen years?'

"The good news is that in Ontario we have begun to implement some consistent training and home study models to help prepare potential adoptive parents: the SAFE home study process and PRIDE training. The two processes are intended to be done concurrently if possible. While PRIDE training is a very valuable process and tool, I think there are a few ways to make it even more effective. It is an important goal to have a common screening and assessment tool for everyone who wants to adopt; there is some value for SAFE being standardized. I think the complication is (looking to what we know about continuing adult education) that the PRIDE curriculum includes a lot of time-sensitive information — that is, at different times during the process of adoptive parenting, from application, placement, and onwards in parenting the adopted child, there are parts of the training information that would be more effective if delivered at the time that it is required by the family. There may be three or four years between taking preparation training and receiving a child in the home. The other challenge is that there is one curriculum for everyone. The attendees could be coming from the positions of fostering a twelve-year-old [or] adopting a newborn to adopting a toddler in Ontario or a six-year-old from Russia. It is a one-size-fits-all program that presents a real challenge to the trainer. He or she must look at the group in front of [him or her] and try to make some accommodations in the delivery of the program, in order to engage everyone across the spectrum."

I ask Michael about how prospective adoptive parents have reacted to the program, as I am aware that it can seem like a never-ending set of application requirements and obstacles. He replies, "Some have said, 'I would not have taken this course had it not been mandatory, but I am glad that I did — all parents should have to take this!'"

Along with the twenty-seven hours of PRIDE training, the home study, and other costs associated with adoption, the cost of applying to adopt a child in Ontario has more than doubled over the last four years. Many couples have already spent thousands of dollars on fertility treatment, and now they must try to cope with not only the exhausting emotional challenges but also the tremendous strain on their finances. I ask Michael if he feels the number of couples seeking adoption has increased in the last ten years.

"There are two things that have evolved: there has been a dramatic decrease in the numbers of newborns available for adoption domestically, and there has been an explosion of people adopting internationally, particularly from China and Russia. In the last eighteen months, however, it is clear that country by country, there is a slowing of the intercountry placement process, an increase in restrictions, and in some cases program stoppages. I feel we have a crisis coming, although life works in large ways. The timing of the baby boom fuelled innovations in infertility technology in the 1980s and '90s, and now we have a blip in thirty-somethings who are ready to parent. Hopefully they will consider Ontario's waiting children."

I ask Michael about new trends in international adoption, specifically with regards to Africa. He begins by saying, "I saw a book recently that is entitled *Africa — The New China?* and currently yes, Africa is the new frontier, and many people seem to be quickly redirecting their efforts to that country, but I am concerned about readiness. These children are national treasures, and as with all international adoptions, if adequate supports could be mobilized to ensure their staying in their country of origin, that would be ideal.

"The problem with these new frontiers in adoption is that, whether we like it or not, there is racial tension that exists in society. Living in Canada we have a hugely more tolerant mindset than other places, but having said that, there is a racial hierarchy that parents have to consider when bringing a child into their homes and communities. The reality is that the thoughts and prejudices about Chinese children are very different from the thoughts and prejudices about black children. I don't know if people are really ready for the different impact that those very real differences will bring — what that child's life is going to be like here as they grow older. It's very sensitive to talk about racial differences and prejudices, but we cannot pretend it doesn't exist. The path in adoption to China has been forged and well defined. The families who have adopted from China, along with the agencies facilitating them, have come together to share their experiences, resources, and support. At a grassroots level, they have planned cultural events and activities that help to provide a transition for their children, but also for the parents — a pathway for getting there, coming back, and going forward in parenting their Chinese child in Canada. With adoptions from Africa, the process will not be so smooth. Parents adopting from Africa will have to be strong advocates for their children and will have to prepare themselves and their children for racial insensitivity."

I am interested to hear Michael's perspectives about domestic adoption and Ontario's waiting children — what can we do?

"There are a great many kids in foster care [about 9,000] in Ontario that need permanent homes, and of them approximately 2,000 to 2,500 are Crown wards (in other words, possibly adoptable). I think what we'll see in the next five to ten years is more domestic placement of these children, if we can get our heads going in the right direction."

At this statement, Michael heaves a deep and contemplative sigh, as he chooses his words carefully.

"There are huge systemic issues, one of which is the paradigm problem. The children in care are being protected by risk managers who have to use a risk management approach in their jobs. They have to think of all the potential downsides, all the ways that things could go wrong; all the ways they must be so careful about this or that. The result can be that the child stays in the system, going back and forth in resource homes. That is not the mentality that is required to place kids or facilitate matching children with permanent families. Placement requires a very different attitude and outlook. The approach has to begin with 'How can we accomplish this?' rather than 'Why we can't do this?' There is a significant difference in the attitude required for the two roles, and I don't know that the same people can do both jobs.

"The next issue is that there are many people who are fostering children, or [who] would consider fostering, who can't afford to adopt those children. Sadly, the moment they adopt them, they lose the drug plan, the subsidies, they lose the payments for psychotherapy or play therapy, they lose the support of the CAS worker, and without those supports they are not able to make the transition and go forward. So those kids stay in limbo for the rest of their growing-up years.

"The solution has to be systemic, and you cannot go down one path of trying to place kids faster without going down the other of providing the support to the adoptive families at the same time. It's an essential piece to a successful placement. It's a problem of too many pockets — the pocket that pays for the foster care, the pocket that pays for continuing services, the pocket that pays for assessing the families — these pockets are all cousins, but they are not [the same]. So we cannot agree to say, 'Okay, we have one funding source, and someone needs to manage this to accomplish what is required for a child regardless of whose pants the pockets are in.' Now how one accomplishes that, with government and fifty-three Children's Aid Societies [in Ontario] with different funding problems and a host of other challenges, that is a big issue. However, addressing this systemic impasse is what would be required in order to fix this.

"If you look at it on a smaller scale, as a family considers adoption via the public system, they will be provided by CAS [with] descriptions and assessments of children available. These could be psychological, casework, or psychiatric assessments, and the way in which the information is presented is not an approach that helps a couple make a decision. Some of the information may have been collected in the investigative phase of the protection hearing. It is risk management or deficit thinking: lists of all the child's problems, diagnoses, medications, and conduct issues. It's not that these things are not significant, but there's no perspective offered that would make an easy bridge for the family to say, 'Okay, if we welcome this child into our family, this is what life is going to be like for us, and there will be supports along the way to help us navigate this.' Perhaps a long meeting with the child's foster parents would be a good early start in the process. They can portray what this child is like on a day-by-day basis and who they are as a person. I think we need a serious think-tank to figure out how we move from the risk management pile over to 'Let's facilitate a family placement in a helpful way that will ensure success for the child and family.' It's that kind of packaging that's needed to make it happen. So some of it is a pocket problem, but a huge amount of it is paradigm shift. This is the kind of issue that requires some minister to have the combination of passion, will, and longevity to accomplish this goal.

"This goal is certainly a shared one in the adoption community, but then people divide very quickly on policies, techniques, and historic approaches, so that's where the conflicts arise. People go back to their particular areas of practice and implement the policies they have been burdened with, and all of a sudden you have huge bridges to cross once again."

Michael breathes another deep sigh and reiterates to me that these are complicated subjects. "You can take the approach that we need the 'great man' in government with the political will and connections to make this happen, or [say] it is the public that needs to get mobilized and pull together the interest groups that want better permanency planning for children," he says. "Some provinces have better organized parent groups than others. In Ontario we do have the population that, with a constituent organization, could represent all the permanency constellations — adoptive parents, foster/resource parents, kinship or grandparent groups — to put pressure on government to effect these changes. Presently we do not have such an organization — at least one that is able to speak in a loud enough, unified voice."

I ask Michael about how our judicial system comes into play around adoption — another complicated subject.

"Over the last few years we have had government focused on child welfare reform. In the beginning one must sell the idea 'Let's transform the way we are doing things. These are important goals; these are Ontario's kids and Ontario's dollars, so let's deliver service better.'

"Then some years are spent working out the mechanics, with one of the results being that the cost of doing an adoption in Ontario has more than doubled. This is all energy downloaded to the private sector — Ontario's public. The original goal was to streamline the home study assessment process — to count people in, not out, and to do more in the recruitment of good families that will accept these kids in need. So now we are in the implementation stage of this, but the budget proposals have come back this way: Children's Aid Societies budgets have been cut or frozen, training budgets have been cut or frozen, and the money that should have gone to child welfare reform is also cut or frozen. So we've shuffled the cards, and it's all great positioning, but the funds aren't there to carry out the real job. Yes, the problems with the courts exist, and I don't think it's going to get better any time soon. There is a backlog of kids at the front end whose families are entering the system, or already there, needing clarity in a timely manner about either remaining in care, going on to a permanency plan, or returning to birth family. There is almost nothing as important in permanency planning as timely disposition of a case. The processing of these cases has not improved, but even if the time frames were shortened, we still don't have the flow-through process in place to put these children anywhere. There are a great many kids who change foster homes in the important first years. We know for certain this delay and uncertainty is not good for kids, never mind not being able to provide them permanent homes. By the time you identify a prospective permanent home, these kids have been through losses and transitions that are going to make a successful permanent placement even more difficult.

"Processing times are critical issues to address, but finding solutions requires dividing the issues into manageable bits. The bits we are talking about are permanency planning, including adoption. Even if the courts were to be transformed next month, we don't have the improvements in place to do anything significant about it.

"One very important component regarding risk management is the issue of control. It's very hard for government to engage in initiatives without having controls in place. But I pointed out earlier … the tremendous initiatives taken by adoptive parents of Chinese children, for example, with respect to resources and ongoing support for each other. It is impossible for control-oriented risk management professionals to appreciate the power of voluntary initiative and harder for them to create and promote it. I don't think the lessons from the initiatives in the private sector in international adoption and in openness in domestic adoption over the last fifteen years were recognized or learned sufficiently in this recent child welfare transformation in Ontario. So in trying to meld private and public adoption together you have a similar problem of control versus initiative and enthusiasm.

"The fact that we now have a common home study assessment process and training model speaks well for consistent screening and preparation, but it puts the brakes on what kind of initiatives can really be brought to bear on this problem of mobilizing public enthusiasm in permanency planning. Post-adoption support groups and resources to support family functioning [and] to provide help when needed must be in place before we can effectively move forward. I am starting to see signs of this in some sectors and hope that these initiatives take hold.

"For example, there are families coming to ask about international adoption who by the end of the assessment and training process are quite ready to consider adopting a child in Ontario. One of the barriers we still see, though, is their difficulty in overcoming feelings of loss in infertility. There is a strong internal struggle with this issue, and sometimes couples desperately want to replace the child they couldn't have — a healthy, perfect infant. It is a hard bridge for them to get over, especially when considering kids with a range of special needs. There are also some illusions about international adoption that are becoming clarified. I talk with couples in these terms: When you foster children, you are presented with a grocery list of problems at the outset. When you adopt a child from a country like Russia or China, you have no information about social or medical family history. But the issues with these children in the next five to ten years won't be that much different than those of a foster child here, except that in the case of international adoption, you have little preparation for what lies ahead. So we have a large presentation problem here. How domestic adoption of older children is positioned, and the readiness of people to see the benefit of this possibility, is going to be what makes the difference if the supports are there.

"In the last five years there have been tremendous advances in the neurosciences; we know what happens in the brains of children who have been exposed to trauma and neglect. And these models can be similarly used to help explain what's happening with kids in foster care or kids in orphanages. When put into these terms, the differences in the children from these two populations are minimal. There's no reason why a couple has to spend forty to fifty thousand dollars to travel around the world to adopt a child, when they could have the satisfaction of parenting a child in need here; that is, as long as we could help them to avoid the nightmare of getting in over their heads by getting into a situation where they have inadequate preparation and no help or support. This shift of attention to Ontario's children shouldn't be that hard to accomplish … except for the problem of pockets. If we could get the pocket problem addressed and focus on getting people what is necessary to do the job and meet these kids' needs — then we could have some very happy kids and happy parents."

Michael and I move on to the topic of open adoption. How is this being viewed by parents and birth families currently?

"There are people who are anxious and worried about openness, but I have found that in the last decade or so, the thinking has moved from token card, letter, and photograph exchanges through a third party to full disclosure and ongoing contact. The Internet and email exchange has been wonderful in this regard.

"People worry about interference in their parenting in contact relationships with birthparents or birth family members. I often say, 'There are a number of people on your street who know your name and where you live — how many of them bother you? So what if you share this info.' It's only in the adoptive parents' mind: that they think they'll be less of a parent if someone else knows this information about them. But I do believe there is a readiness in openness in our communities about open adoption that wasn't there twenty years ago. Proper preparation, and knowing what this really looks like on the ground, allows people to make the shift to openness. As long as people can participate in a respectful process and feel they can control their role as a parent and a person, then everyone is happy. I think the move towards openness is not meeting with much resistance. In the vast majority of cases, disclosure doesn't present problems. There are a few situations when someone shouldn't have contact with someone else, and if we have a vehicle to handle that privacy then openness is a good thing. The more people talk about their experience of openness in adoption, the more it helps others to cross that bridge."

Finally, I ask Michael to talk about the social stigma that still exists surrounding adoption in our society today. How can we move beyond the perceptions of the past?

Michael begins by stating, "Nobody likes adoption. By that, I mean that underlying it all, there's some criticism and discomfort about it [a birthparent not parenting their child]. From the professional or bureaucratic point of view, this [placing of a child] is an unnatural thing, a designer option that we've invented. The point of view is that it shouldn't be happening in the first place, so we fiddle with it using controls and requirements that make it as long, arduous, and difficult a process as possible. In fact, many policy makers or adoption thinkers I meet don't have a love or appreciation for the core process of putting a home together for a kid and a family. It's very hard to get clear thinking from the start, on the deepest level of this issue, when this kind of fundamental prejudice is underlying the whole mechanism.

"As a result, the members of the adoption constellation are left to grapple with their part in it without the support they deserve. People who have been going through years of infertility have little support because people are shy about this loss and don't know what to say. It's very difficult for birthparents to get the help they need because placing a child is a shame-based issue and again no one knows what to say — and when they do, it's usually 'How could you give up your child, I could never do that?' And then it's hard for adopted children to get support from peers because they don't want to come out and be different — they want to be like every other kid.

"There's a lot of research coming out now on what are called 'before factors.' These factors are things like the mom's emotional state while she was pregnant, what that does to her chemistry; the stress levels and what impact that has on the fetus; what kind of drugs [and] environmental exposures has this mom experienced or exposed the child to. The impact of these factors can be found in long-term societal demands on health care, on social [work], and [on] the education systems to deal with Fetal Alcohol Syndrome, ADHD, and other emotional or cognitive delays. So people who may be opposed to adoption as a process cannot respond to questions such as, Why can't we help these birthmoms; give them social supports; help them have a happy, healthy pregnancy; longer paid leave to look after their kids, to launch kids properly? And there is a dollar cost that can be measured of not providing these supports. If I said to the government, 'This mom is walking around in the winter with no coat — can we buy her a coat?' the answer would be no, we can't give moms who are planning adoption placement anything material. If you really believe in the impact of these 'before factors' then we should be helping the mom in every way necessary to ensure a healthy pregnancy and birth — otherwise all the pockets are going to pay for this child down the road. But it's like thinking the unthinkable, to do anything significantly helpful for this mom in the pregnancy phase, because we run into the control problem of what if she's influenced, what if she's bribed, what if she's paid? No one wants to be seen to be interfering in the birthparent's decision to keep or to place her child. In maintaining this attitude, we fall over backwards to be abstinent and therefore we neglect the mom and the child's needs … most importantly, the child is already off to an uncertain start."

And with that Michael has to quit. He tells me he could talk for three more hours on this subject, but I realize I have already delayed his next appointment. He goes back to doing the business of his life — matching parents with children — and I walk out of his office into the pouring rain, my thoughts swirling with the impact of all he has said. If only we would all listen to what he has to say, and then act.

Personal collection of Brenda McCreight.

Brenda McCreight

Therapist and Counsellor
Adoptive Mother

WHEN I WAS with the Gilbert family in Nanaimo, where Brenda McCreight lives, I did not have the privilege of interviewing her in person. Brenda was out of town speaking at one of the many workshops, conferences, and other activities that account for some of the time she devotes to her career as a child and family therapist, counsellor, and coach. Her expertise is in helping children and families who are facing such issues as sexual abuse and family violence, as well as adoption and foster care concerns.

Brenda is very well qualified to be doing this work from an academic perspective and, most importantly, from a personal perspective. She is the mother of fourteen children, twelve whom are adopted and are considered to have special needs.

Brenda managed to answer a few of my questions about her perspectives on adoption in Canada by email. I asked Brenda about an adoptive family's greatest need.

"Since 1982, I have been counselling all members of the adoption family — basically, whoever calls. I don't know the percentages, but at least 60 percent are families with children who have highly disruptive and challenging behaviours. These families need appropriate support from adoption specialized professionals. This would include respite, therapy, marital counselling, family therapy, and child therapy.

"Presently in Canada there are not enough resources available. Only a handful of universities include adoption training in their social work programs, and there is nothing about adoption in education or medical programs. Therefore resources are developed, such as treatment centres, that don't include programs or methods that would suit a psychologically or emotionally challenged child who has a functioning and capable family. Unfortunately, because I work all over the U.S., Canada, and the U.K., I can tell you the situation is the same everywhere."

I asked Brenda where the first place to start would be. "Respite would be a main priority, to help alleviate the exhaustion that so many parents experience. Therapists and youth workers who have been trained in adoption would be a second choice," she said.

Since the majority of Brenda's work involves helping families with children with special needs, I asked about lessons she has learned form her own experiences.

"I have learned that children with challenges are also children with gifts and joy. They change the life of the adoptive family in ways one never expected or even knew could happen. They make us look at ourselves and at the world in new colours and new dimensions, and they teach us not only to think outside of the box, but to realize that there never was a box, that we have the power to create everything we need to make our lives better. There is a saying that 'God is in the details,' and I believe that they force us to live in the details, so that we have a richer, more profound experience of life that we would have ever had without them."

The following is an article Brenda wrote for *Family Helper*. It is full of wisdom and reassurances for families facing the challenge of children with special needs — but frankly it can apply to any of us with children who are just trying to figure it all out. If you go to Brenda's website, www.theadoptioncounsellor.com, you can get a daily dose of common sense when your life is in dire need of it. Thank you, Brenda.

Article for Family Helper

I have been a child and family therapist for twenty-five years (when did I get that old?). In my therapeutic and coaching practice, I work with adoptive and foster parents to help them develop strategies for managing children with the challenging behaviours that are associated with attachment trauma, FASD, ADHD, anger management, and simply learning how to belong to a loving family. In B.C., all adoptions must be done through either the government services or through a licensed B.C. agency, and so the families I work with have adopted through the government adoption services, which only place waiting children from the B.C. foster care system; and I work with those who have adopted through licensed agencies, which facilitate international adoptions of infants, toddlers, and children from foreign orphanages or from the foster care system in the U.S.

It never ceases to amaze me how, once the decision has been made to adopt domestically, people start to creep out of the woodwork with tales of horror and woe about children adopted from the public system. Suddenly everyone can tell you a story about some child from _____ (fill in the blank, although it's usually some southern U.S. state), who terrorized his adoptive parents and ruined their lives. I even had a hairdresser start to tell me how his adopted nephews tried to kill their mother, and he was telling the story while cutting my daughter's hair! Most children who are adopted from the public system are not newborns by the time they are placed. They will have had many significant life problems to deal with long before their first birthday. Each and every day that they were ignored, or hurt, or left to feel abandoned will have caused a degree of damage that the adoptive parents will have to heal. And it's true that the process of healing takes time and energy and resources that the adoptive parent may not have anticipated. But is that enough to forgo the experience?

Recently, I have been hearing people say, "Adoption isn't for the faint of heart." I take umbrage with that (I am not sure what umbrage is, but it is such a great-sounding word that I am sure I would take it if I knew the meaning). Let's face it, life isn't for the faint of heart. Even those who have not adopted challenging children have tough times in their lives (look at poor Britney Spears, all that money and she still can't find clothes that fit!). So, I think we should stop moaning about how tough it is to raise challenging children and start focusing on how lucky we are to have them. I know … if you are in the middle of a crisis right now, it will be hard to think how this could be called luck. Well, stand back a minute and look at your life again. This child, rages and all, has given you the opportunity to be a parent, and that is what you wanted. He has also given you the opportunity to learn new ways of talking and listening, new ways of relating, new ways to value your relationships, and maybe some new friends (okay, so the police officer that caught him stealing last Thursday isn't a friend yet, but trust me, a couple of years from now he will be your best buddy). Your child has moved you from complacency to valuing every moment that is good in your life; and from smugness to humility.

Our children start off in our families with some real issues. The hardest for many is that they have to do all their learning about how to be a child and how to belong to a family in their growing-up years, instead of in infancy when they were supposed to. That means the adoptive family is going to go through stages where the "tough" part overwhelms the "rewards" part. So, what are some simple strategies to help you hang in there till the rewarding times start to overtake the tough times (yes, they will). Well, after being a therapist for twenty-five years and an adoptive parent for twenty-four years, here's what I think it comes down to:

1. Focus on changing yourself, not the child. He is just who he is, tantrums, lying, and all. You are the functional, intelligent adult, and you have the ability to learn new ways of parenting. Once you have done that, he will be able to learn new ways of being a child.

2. Live your life as if the problems (remember, I said the problems, not the child) didn't exist. Don't focus every day, and every decision, on Junior. Because, as we all know, Junior is going to come out of this just fine eventually, and there is no point putting your life on a shelf for two years, or getting divorced, while he sets a new standard for "attitude."

3. Get enough sleep at least four times a week. If you have to, take shifts, or once in a while hire a babysitter while you nap.

4. Get an updated psychological assessment (on the child, not you) as well as blood tests and allergy tests. It may be "older child adoption issues," or it may be that Junior was never properly assessed for his needs as a younger child. Psychology is an ever-changing field, and problems that were not well understood when you adopted Junior may be more easily addressed now.

5. Learn and use conflict resolution skills. Formal conflict resolution skills really work. They won't change Junior, but they will change how you engage in the argument and how you feel about yourself afterward.

6. Find a way to enjoy at least an hour with Junior once a week; once a day if possible (but if that was possible, you wouldn't be reading this article). Take him out for a fast food lunch and just let him talk on, and on, and on … without benefit of your advice or opinion (I bet your parents did that with you). It won't change anything, and it might raise your blood pressure, but it will help you to know him in the present and give you something good to think about when you are lying awake worrying about the meeting with his teacher tomorrow.

7. Find a hobby or interest that makes you feel good. Take a couple of hours a week to focus on you, not on Junior.

8. Let the rest of the children have a "normal" family life. Take vacations without Junior so that the siblings still get to have a childhood. Don't miss their soccer games just because Junior came home stoned, he's only going to sleep anyway, so leave the argument till later and go cheer the one who is still behaving.

9. Believe in your child and your family. Your belief that your family can make it and that Junior will be okay again, someday, are often all that our children have as a guiding light to that destination. They want to get there too, despite what it looks like now.

10. Remind yourself that this will pass. As someone once said, "Everything works out in the end, and if it hasn't worked out, then it isn't the end." Twelve-year-olds are in process, they are not finished. Neither are you!

Photo by Julian Katz.

Michael Grand
PhD

**Psychologist and Professor,
University of Guelph
Step-Adoptee**

DR. MICHAEL GRAND has a lot to say about adoption, and when he talks, people listen. He himself is a step-adoptee and has spent his career as a psychologist (and currently a professor at the University of Guelph) doing research, writing, and speaking all over North America on the subject. He was a co-director of the National Adoption Study of Canada, one of the biggest and most comprehensive of its kind. The study included all the provinces and territories of Canada, and it collected and documented data on adoption rules, regulations, practices, and legislation. Michael's public speaking record is at least five times as long as his publications, as he admittedly likes to take his research to the street. His driving passion is open adoption at every level — in placement, facilitation, and the ongoing life of the adoptive family. He has been very involved in the debates in the Ontario legislature regarding opening records for adoptees and birth families to be granted easier access to their biological past. I meet with Michael in his office on the campus of University of Guelph for what is one of the most enlightening ninety-minute talks I have ever had, learning more about his life's work. He begins by talking about some concerns he has in adoption trends.

"With Internet use so prevalent, I am very concerned that many adoption websites are geared towards assisting couples in adopting children, and in the service of that goal, they have in essence turned their backs on the experience of those who are giving birth to these children. The best example I can give of that is through indirect evidence. When you go on some of these websites you'll see that they are decorated with hearts and flowers and lots of pink, warm, fuzzy baby stuff, in their attempts to solicit the cooperation of potential birthparents. What those sites never do is talk about the experience for birthparents post-placement. One of the reasons why I have supported open adoption is because it recognizes and legitimizes the feelings of the birthparent and goes some distance to ameliorate some of the complex feelings of loss of control, helplessness, and depression about the future, in that it will never bring an end to the feelings of loss. I say that tentatively because for some birthparents, even in the best of adoptions, they forever feel the loss. They have to live with that every day. Open adoption at least gives them some opportunity for repair work around that. I don't know if it does completely, but I think it goes some way in trying to address a problem which those websites turn their backs on. These people are making very courageous decisions.

"I think one of the key words in successful adoptions is the word *empathy*. It's empathy for all parties to the adoption. There has to be empathy for the need of the adoptee and their fantasies about their birth family, or when they say, 'You're not my real mom' or all the other things that can take place in an adoption … to understand what that means. And the feelings of knowing you started out in one womb and ended up in another 'room.' In somebody else's 'room,' and to be able to understand what that means. To empathize with someone who's trying to sort out 'Who am I?' is an absolute need. I think adoptees need the sense of empathy, which they can only learn from their adoptive parents — for the experience of their parents, who have not had biological children, [for] what their experience means and why they invest so much in it (sometimes too much, [although] not with the intent of trying to harm). Sometimes adoptive parents work so hard to make that child into their biological child, when the real empathy they need with that child is to recognize that their child has a unique genetic makeup, which may not allow that child to be a reflection of themselves. Nevertheless, the child can be their psychological child.

"There's empathy for the needs of the birthparents. If the adoptive parents can't show empathy for the birthparents, they will translate a message to the child about the inadequacies of the birthparent. And here's where the great paradox comes. By disparaging the actions of the birthparent, they will end up disparaging the DNA of the child. They will push their child away from them and create a greater emotional distance from them. One of the studies I conducted found that when adoptive parents speak ill of the birthparents, the child actually identifies more strongly with the birthparents. For adoptive parents, it's the perfect way to push their children away if they bad-mouth their child's origins. I understand that some adoptive parents do this in the service of trying to say to the child, 'I really love you, and maybe your birthparents weren't showing the same kind of compassion for you' — but that is not how the message is heard, and in the end it isn't empathy for a combination of social circumstances by which a woman has to have her child placed into someone else's home.

"I believe the easiest way to understand adoption is to understand paradox. Whatever you think it is, it's usually the opposite. The more adoptive parents try to push away birth family, the more birth family will have a prominent place in the mind of the adoptee. The more adoptive parents respect the child's origins, the less birth family will fill a threatening emotional space in the life of the adoptive parents. The more adoptive parents can embrace that understanding, the closer will the child come to them. If you block out that reality, the more they push the child away. That is a great paradox."

Michael has been trying to get this message across in many ways, through research, articles, speaking, radio, and newspapers, but he says that changing public ways of talking about things takes a long time. One of the things he recently found interesting was during the court case in late 2007 that sadly struck down bill 183. "The judge used the term *adoption constellation*, a term that I authored to replace the word *triad*. The triad, which has been used commonly in adoption, to me is the biggest distortion one can have of what's going on in adoption because it says that the birthparent, adoptee, and adoptive parent are in an equilateral relationship in this triad. Yet we know that people have different degrees of power at different times, and they are not necessarily equal in any way. The constellation recognizes that a large number of systemic relationships with individuals outside of the nuclear adoptive family shift over time with changing emotional gravitational pull between members of the constellation. There are also black holes of silence and secrecy. Throughout, there are opportunities for different parts of the constellation to be illuminated or made more salient at different times in the life of the adopted family. I think we're changing some of the language, and the language changes the way we think about adoptive relationships."

I ask Michael where the birthfather fits into this constellation.

"I've never been able to find the source of this statistic, and it may not be correct, but I have been told that 25 percent of birthmothers don't know who the birthfather is, 25 percent know who the birthfather is but have not told him he is the father, and then the remainder [50 percent] know. To begin with we cut one half of the birthfathers out, because they have no way of knowing that they are the birthfathers. And then beyond that group, we've instituted practices in adoption that have kept him at bay. And in our society, unfortunately, men have not been the most responsible creatures, in terms of stepping up to the mark. Where I come from, it takes two to tango, and kids that end up in adoption don't result from an immaculate conception! We don't hear very much from birthfathers. There's a little bit of change with regards to signing consents as birthmothers do. Also, birthdads historically have not been overwhelmingly great in reunion — in either accepting paternity or fostering a relationship with the adoptee.

"People will not like to hear me say this, but the attitude about birthdads in our society is reflective of a pervasive attitude in adoption, that what is important is to find a child for adoptive parents … and only secondarily a home for an adopted child. It shouldn't be in that order, but it is, which means that you then ignore any impediments to finding a child for adoptive parents, and what are the impediments: the impediments are recognizing that there may be other options for a birthmom besides placement, and the potential impediment of involving the other parent — the birthfather. If you ignore the interests and needs of these two, you speed up the process of placing the child. However, in doing so, we fail to address the most important player in the whole system, the child, who is the person in the weakest position of all. In the end, we shouldn't be turning our backs on anyone."

Michael's personal experience of being a step-adoptee has helped him navigate the field through a unique perspective. His father died when he was six years old, and a few years later, when his mother remarried, he was adopted by her second husband. His name was changed, and his records were sealed so that his modified long form birth registration says that he is the biological child of his adoptive father. In essence, the document says that he is not the biological child of the man who fathered him and who parented him for six years. He grew up in a closed adoption, which meant that they never discussed his biological father after his adoption. It was as if his mother's second husband was to become that father to him. Michael's younger brother didn't know he was adopted for a few years after the fact.

"It took all of us a while to sort out what was going on. I still had a remembrance of my father — my brother didn't. Step-adoptees lack two major things — they live with one biological parent, but the parent may follow the advice of professionals and engage in the myth that the adoptive parent is, in fact, the biological parent. The other issue is that they don't think of themselves as adoptees, they don't have that identity-label of adoptee. When I did a study about step-adoption, every adoptee told me that until they saw my research poster, they had never thought of themselves as an adoptee. But what was very fascinating was that everything that makes or doesn't make for a successful full adoption is exactly the same for step-adoptions, including access to the other parent and the other parent's kids. I have one foot outside adoption and one foot inside, and I think it has helped me to be more knowledgeable on a gut level [regarding] what adoption is about, and it's given me a little bit of distance to provide the more scientific rigour of trying to keep my own agenda off the table as I try and look at what the phenomena are all about."

Michael has had the opportunity to meet several birth families in reunion and was amazed to see the physical and intellectual similarities between adoptees and birth relatives. They had overlapping characteristics that were astounding. "To be able to ground yourself in history is so affirming," he says.

"One of the things we found in our research is that the more adoptive parents support the search without guilt, the closer they bring themselves to their adult child. The more they reject the search, try to hold on to the child as their child, the more the child is drawn away, towards the birth family. They will stay much closer to you if you say, 'I know you have to go on this journey, and I'm here to support you whatever happens. I'm here with you and love you.' Why do we need to be so possessive of our love for a child? There can't be too much love in the world. If we share it, the child's heart is filled with even more. You don't have to love the other family, just as you may not love your in-laws, but you know that there are certain forms of behaviour that you have to engage in to be able to keep your relationship with your spouse. This is almost the equivalent case. It is the family that is able to have more flexible boundaries around these relationships that is going to succeed."

I ask Michael what his thoughts are on same-sex, single-parent, and interracial adoptions.

"My concern is much more with the process than with the players. It has to do with the quality of relationships between people — why are they adopting, are they making lifelong commitments to this child that they are bringing into their life, and will they have respect for that child's origin. Where I do have concerns is regarding egg or sperm donation and now embryo donation. I've spoken with lesbian couples who have said, 'We do not want to have any involvement with the sperm source in our lives so there is no way we are going to have an open relationship with the man who donated the sperm.' Unfortunately, it's just the same old nonsense all over again that we've faced in adoption. There's no desire to recognize the need of the child to know one's origins."

With a view to international adoption, Michael asks, "What is the motivation for adopting from overseas? I do accept our research finding that some people go overseas because they can expedite an adoption much more quickly. That being said, others adopt from overseas because they think they can avoid what they see as the problem of the interfering birth family. The bottom line is that psychologically they never will remove the birth family; they will create a situation that heightens the salience of the birth family.

"I have great empathy for children who are growing up in the worst of circumstances overseas, and anything we can do to improve the quality of their life should be done. One of those things may be adoption. But before you get to adoption internationally, we should be looking at a very different set of questions. What can we in the West do to improve the circumstances in the home country so that it is not necessary for that child to be uprooted? I've met too many international adult adoptees who have said to me, 'I feel like an orphan in history — I'm neither Chinese nor am truly accepted in Canada'; they feel like they're neither fish nor fowl, and they really struggle with who they are in the world. The only group that's been well researched is the Korean adoptees who, came to the U.S. in the 1970s and '80s. Many came with a full identifying history, so we are now seeing reunions taking place. You can imagine what it's like when you come from a First World adoptive family and you go back to a Third World birth family. It's a huge cultural jump, and whether people are able to make that leap is very challenging; it takes very special people to be able to do it."

Michael shares his thoughts about the critical issues in adoption.

"My driving passion is open adoption at every level — placement, in the ongoing life of the adoptive family, and in search, reunion, and reconnection. It is also fundamental to change legislation to unseal the records and give people the right to access their own private information. I think until we do that, adoption will always be mired in all the difficulties we've talked about. The issue of openness drives everything else from beginning to end. Out of that, there are other kinds of needs for improvement, like public education. There is a huge need for training of a new kind of professional in adoption who understands the realities of the dynamics of the adoption constellation. Without that, I fear for the future of adoption, because we simply continue to perpetuate the past while playing lip service to needs for openness."

If adoptive families are beginning to embrace openness more, I ask how they would be able to navigate through it — Support? Education? "We have to think about who is doing adoption and who is facilitating it. Are they truly open to this agenda, and I'm not certain they really are."

I ask him why it has taken so many attempts at trying to get the disclosure bill passed to even come close to being successful. He answers, "The sad thing is that a well-gathered fact never gets in the way of a strongly held opinion. Somehow or other, everyone is an expert on adoption. I have never heard so many strongly held opinions — everyone thinks they know about adoption, but they don't map on to the reality of the lived experience of people. Sandra Pupatello was the first minister of Community and Social Services out of the five that I met who, when I walked into the room and started my pitch for why the law should be changed, put her hand up and said, 'You don't have to convince me why; let's talk about how.' She really got it. That was then.

"The bill now has been modified by the court decision that I find to be a highly flawed decision. It is based on innuendo and fear. All of the arguments were based on one main issue — that being that if the records were opened, all hell would break loose. In countries such as Britain, Scotland, Scandinavia, Israel, and five U.S. states, the records have been opened, and as far as I know, the world has not come to a standstill because of it. The politicians were painting a picture of destroyed families. This is not the case. Most adoptees and birth families are so terrified of being rejected that they approach this task so gingerly and tentatively that most sit on it for long periods of time before they start the process. People need to put it in place and think what it will mean to them."

What are the characteristics of good adoptive parents?

"One of the most important revelations to me through my studies is that what makes a good adoptive parent is also what makes a good biological parent. They really are not far apart. It is acknowledging the difference between oneself and one's child and nurturing the unique qualities of the child, as opposed to saying, 'If the child is not like me, the child has no worth.' That is such an important quality in good parenting; it's the same quality that's necessary in adoption. It's the acknowledgement of differences. You also have to have openness and respectful conversation. These are all the qualities of good parenting. When adoptive parents believe that adopting a child is identical to having a biological child, they are looking for legitimacy instead of being able to celebrate difference. And that's very sad, because I think in the end with that kind of attitude, they will not succeed in the role of good adoptive parents. One of the reasons that they seek legitimacy is that many adoptive parents who have not had biological children experience what has been called 'disenfranchised grief' — it's grief that isn't acknowledged, the grief of not being able to have a child. If you get to adopt a child, with each subsequent stage in development the parents are reminded of the child they didn't have. They can't express that sense of loss because to do so would be seen to be turning their back on the adoptee. So they have to bear this grief in silence, without social support, as they try to push away the grief of not being able to be a biological parent. In the counselling of adoptive families, professionals must recognize the losses of all members of the constellation. I don't get caught up in whose grief is more important, but we need to acknowledge it and then be able to do something to lessen it. In many adoption-related support groups, these things are never dealt with. All that is discussed is 'How do we deal with this difficult child.' So there is a need for counsellors who truly understand the dynamics of adoption and the needs of everyone in the constellation."

Michael believes the language we use in adoption is an important factor in changing perceptions and attitudes around the subject of adoption. "Respectful communication is one of the foundations for successful parenting, and that means that you don't belittle, and you don't say, 'I've saved you from a fate worse than death — and you don't appreciate what I've given you.'"

He summarizes what he calls the most important things for people to understand about adoption with openness as the foundation.

"Openness is acknowledgement of difference, celebration of difference as opposed to the denial of differences; the importance of respect for all parties in the constellation — respect for adoptive parents who have been belittled by people who have been hurt by adoption, respect for adoptees who are struggling to find out who they are and are impeded at every turn, respect for birthparents, many of whom had no choice in the decisions that were made about their children."

I ask for his perspectives on birthparents who do not wish any contact with their children, and he says, "As sad as I think that is, because in the end I think even a bad reunion is more healing than no reunion, I believe people have to make that decision for themselves. Everyone is entitled to a history — but no one is entitled to a relationship. We all should have the right to know where we've come from or what happened to our children. That's what's so unbelievably frustrating about sealed records. Your history is in a file in a government warehouse, and you don't have a right to know who you are — yet every other citizen has the right to know one's personal information …

"Politicians and editorialists talk about adoptees and birthparents as if they were pathological criminals, saying they can't be trusted and should not have the same right to that same document — it's just bizarre to me — crazy …"

And I echo the sentiment — crazy.

Marilyn Churley

Former MPP New Democratic Party
Birthmother and Adoption Disclosure
Advocate

Personal collection of Marilyn Churley.

THERE ARE A few things that I think I can expect about Marilyn Churley before we meet at her East York home. I know that she will not be at a loss for words, and that her words will be served straight up.

She is a woman of conviction, and, as illustrated in her political career, she does not suffer fools or back down from a challenge. There's one other thing I'm fairly sure of — that I will like her, and by the end of our conversation about her role in the adoption disclosure legislation, I am correct on both counts. Marilyn begins with a little history.

"In 1979, Ontario became the leader in North America of bringing in Canada's first adoption disclosure registry. It was a passive registry, whereby both parties, birth families and adoptees, would apply to seek connection and then wait. The system quickly became backlogged, and some people waited over ten years to actually be given the information, and then only non–identifying information."

Marilyn's personal experience as a young woman in 1968, relinquishing her baby boy for adoption, was certainly a factor in motivating her to seek change in the legislation. In 1990, Marilyn's election to the Ontario legislature would begin a long and arduous journey towards adoption legislation reform.

"Although in the beginning there was not a lot of opposition to my efforts to convince my cabinet to sponsor a bill, it wasn't until the late 1990s that I could devote the time and effort it would take to bring a bill forward. I worked at bringing members of the adoption community together, such as COAR [Coalition for Open Adoption Records], Parent Finders, and the Adoption Council of Canada, to help support the bill. Tony Martin, then M.P.P. from Sault Ste. Marie, agreed to sponsor the private member's bill with the backing of Premier Bob Rae and his cabinet. The legislative process is so time-consuming that by the time the bill [after having passed second reading] was read for the final vote, it was the last day of the house sitting in December 1998. We thought we had an agreement with the opposition that the bill would pass, but two opposition members, Jim Bradley and Norm Sterling, filibustered, talked the clock out, and the bill died on the Order Paper. We were devastated. Each and every time in the next five years of reintroducing four more private member's bills we would devote an enormous amount of work that included press conferences, phone calls, mailings, and meetings with staff and the adoption community. The truth is that very few members of the legislature understood the true importance of the bill or the extent to which it affected the public. Some were willing to be educated, but most fell to influences of preconceived and misguided notions about adoption and [to] the media's desire to sensationalize the issue."

In June of 2000, Bill 108 died after only one reading, but the following year Bill 77 gave more promise.

"After Bill 77 passed second reading, after much grovelling and lobbying I got approval from the government and the opposition parties to let the bill go to public hearings at Queen's Park. We had strong support from professional members of the adoption community, Children's Aid, as well as from Dr. Phillip Wyatt, who was Chief of Genetics at North York General Hospital. He wrote a letter arguing the physiologically based importance of opening birth records, in that there are over 2,500 inheritable diseases that Ontarians could be affected by, unbeknownst to them or to their offspring."

Privacy Commissioners in other jurisdictions that reformed adoption disclosure in Canada had objected to the retroactivity aspects of reform, and Marilyn was worried that

Ontario's Privacy Commissioner, Ann Cavoukian, might have the same objections. Adoption disclosure legislation was not even under her jurisdiction, but Marilyn knew that her opinion could kill the bill, so in advance of the hearings Marilyn met with her in an attempt to persuade her to support the bill. Unfortunately, not only did Cavoukian decide to oppose the bill, she became a powerful and vocal public voice against it.

"She had the right to her opinion, however, and unfortunately it was enough to influence Premier Ernie Eves' decision to back down. The government got cold feet, and a letter from Ann Cavoukian, expressing that she could not support the bill, effectively killed it. It was March 18, 2003."

On May 15 of the same year, Marilyn's fourth private member's bill, Bill 16, passed second reading. This time it was in competition with Progressive Conservative Wayne Wettlaufer's Bill 60. The two bills both called for the same disclosure, but the fines related to non-compliance with a no contact order by either an adoptee or birth family were vastly different. Wettlaufer's proposal was a $100,000 fine to Marilyn's $10,000 fine. Premier Eves called a provincial election on September 2, 2003, bringing an end to Parliament and effectively killing both bills. I ask Marilyn how she persevered throughout all of the frustrations.

"My personal experience of reuniting with my birthson in 1996 was what fuelled my passion. It was only through my own efforts that I was able to connect with my son. Even if I did not want contact with him, would I have the right to prevent my son from accessing information about himself? Certainly not. One has to put [oneself] in the place of adoptees … above everyone. Think about the implications of having your personal history locked away in some vault. Besides, I have always maintained the caveat that everyone has the right to personal information, not to a relationship."

In 2003, when Premier Dalton McGuinty and the Liberals took power, Marilyn once again started the process to introduce her fifth bill, Bill 14. Sandra Pupatello was the Minister of Community and Social Services and was very keen to be as informed as possible about the issues surrounding the bill. The bill was introduced to the opposition, which was then led by John Tory.

"During the public hearings, with Clayton Ruby in attendance, Ann Cavoukian put on an almost tearful display of emotion, claiming to represent the voiceless and using letters from people who did not want to be identified, describing sensational and controversial stories involving incest and rape. I was flabbergasted at the behaviour, but it resulted in her desired effect. It gave the opposition the ammunition they needed to keep up the fight against its passage and created a negative media backlash against the bill."

To the minister's and government's credit, the bill did pass, but in came lawyer Clayton Ruby, who launched a constitutional challenge that prevented the bill's implementation.

"I sat in the courtroom every day with some of the leaders of COAR and watched all our hard work unravel. Mr. Ruby was representing four people, two adult adoptees and a birthmother and birthfather, all of whom wanted a disclosure veto included in the bill. On the first day, to our astonishment, the judge declared to Mr. Ruby, 'You have the hardest case to win,' and then told him chapter and verse what he had to do to ensure that indeed he would win. And win he did. The government decided not to appeal the decision, so the bill was dead. I think we might have won on an appeal. Some birthmothers may have been told that their anonymity would be safeguarded, but there was never anything in writing, and I still maintain that it is a moral issue. Adult adoptees should be allowed to have the same personal information about themselves that the rest of us take for granted. When I look back at the ten-plus years of leading the legislative efforts on this issue, I find it interesting that most of the opposition came from men. It would make one wonder what ghosts were lurking in whose closets. Perhaps some were afraid they'd get the mythical dreaded knock on the door. What evidence shows is that the knock rarely — if ever — happens. The men would always speak up to protect the birthmothers, and I would remind them, 'I am a birthmother!' The adoption of a child and all the people it affects is a life journey. Locking it away in a closet and keeping it a secret hurts all concerned. It really comes down to human rights … the right of an adoptee to know his or her personal information and the right of birthparents to know what happened to their children."

At this writing, the adoption disclosure bill has been reintroduced as Bill 183 with a contact veto. There are a few things in the bill that still concern Marilyn. Sadly, the government has also decided to discontinue the adoption disclosure registry, presumably to save money, which the adoption community vehemently opposes. Marilyn Churley remains passionate and committed to continuing public and media education surrounding adoption disclosure. The media has proclaimed her "mother of the bill," and while she is proud to have been instrumental in its progress, and in coming a long way to seeing greater understanding not only in government but also by the public, her even greater pride is in the treasured role of mother to Bill, the son she once lost and then finally found. When Marilyn Churley tells her story, I predict it will go a long way to encouraging others to muster the same courage. The courage to embrace the truth …the courage to heal.

Note: Adoption Disclosure Bill 12 was passed in May 2008, and it includes a contact veto.

Afterword

AFTER SHARING IN my glimpse of the Canadian families and adoption professionals in *Labours of Love*, my hope is that you have gained insight into the complex but truly inspiring journey of adoption. Unless you have personally experienced this journey by being a member of the "adoption constellation," as Michael Grand so aptly describes it, it is impossible to understand completely the feelings of those whose lives are forever influenced by adoption.

I would ask only this of you: When you are confronted with the concept of adoption, whether through the media, family, friends, work associates, or strangers, remain open to listening without judgment, speaking with empathy, and, above all, remembering that we are all children of the world, deserving of understanding, love, and compassion. Hold the children in your heart.

Deborah A. Brennan

Letter to Prospective Adoptive Parents from a Birthmother

Tara Nielson

Dear Prospective Adoptive Parents,

I have been asked to share with you what I, as a birthmother, wish adoptive parents knew. It is difficult for me to find the right words to describe the many things I wish adoptive parents knew. I became a birthmother almost five years ago and now have a wonderful relationship with my son, Thomas, and his adoptive family. This relationship has taken a lot of hard work, honesty, communication, and trust. Some of what I write may be hard to read. It is not my intention to scare or shock you, but to educate you. My hope is that this letter will assist you as you continue in your adoption journey.

Just as each person is different, each birthparent is different. There is not one specific thing or a list of specific qualities that each potential birthparent looks for when finding parents for his or her child. Many birthparents look for families who practise a specific religion or who have similar racial or cultural backgrounds as themselves. I wanted to find parents who were like me — liked to travel, liked to "play," had similar values and beliefs, as well as many other qualities. I chose parents for my son because they seemed to parent like I thought I might one day.

After I placed my son for adoption I learned some truths about open adoption that I would like to share with you. Firstly, open adoption relationships are hard work and require a lot of commitment. Birthparents love their children and want the best for them. Please know that birthparents do not place their children for adoption to make your family complete. They place them because they want to make their child complete. We consider you, the parents, to be a gift for our child, not the other way around.

You might become fearful and question their intentions when your child's birthparents want to visit with your child frequently or call frequently in the beginning. Please understand that in the beginning most birthparents are unsure that they have made the right decision. I know my mind wondered frequently, *Have I made the right choice?* Most birthparents call or visit frequently not because they desire to intrude or disrupt, but because they find peace in their decision when they can see how much you love your child.

During visits or phone calls your child's birthparents may become emotional, especially in the beginning. The harsh reality of open adoption is that the birthparents hurt and grieve. It will not be easy to watch your child's birthparent as they grieve. You might question the benefits of your open adoption agreement. You might think it is too hard for your child's birthparents — that maybe you should take a step back. Do not think that it would be easier for your child's birthparents if you cut off contact with them. When it comes to their child, most birthparents did not seek the easy route, but instead they sought what was best for their child. Please do not jump to conclusions about the birthparents' emotions. They are capable of knowing when they need to step back.

Promises are sacred. Please keep your promises for contact and visitation even when you are scared. Open adoption should not be based on the adoptive parents' or the birthparents' fluctuating feelings. Open adoption is for your child. Your fear is a reason, not an excuse. Never think your child's birthparents are not and were not afraid. As they place their child into your waiting arms they are terrified! When you think of all they have asked of you, think for a moment what you have asked of them — their child.

People will question your "realness" as a parent, and you may tell them, "I am the one who changes diapers, kisses booboos, and buys her clothes; therefore I am the real parent." Please know that most birthparents do not place their children because they could not change a diaper. We can wake up in the middle of the night for feedings, we can kiss booboos, and even though money is often tight, we can buy clothing. Both the birth and adoptive parents are "real," but by placing our children for adoption we have given you permission to be the parents. By recognizing the birthparents' role in your child's life, you lose nothing, but we all gain so much.

Birthparents place their children with adoptive families because you can give the child what they could not at that given time. They can provide them with shelter, but often not direction. They are often still struggling to find their own way in life. They can give hugs, but often not proper discipline. They are often still trying to find order in their own lives. They can give their child love, but they often cannot give their child the best.

Claiming to be the "real" parent takes away from one and gives to another. Do not tear down your child's birthparents and belittle their sacrifices in order to build yourself up. You have sacrificed, and birthparents thank you, but they signed their parental rights away, not the right to love their child and not their right to be their child's parent by birth.

This letter was written in hopes of giving other birthparents a voice and to help you understand birthparents better. Of course, I do not claim to speak for all birthparents. Each has their own story and they have a right to tell it. All too often birthparents remain silent, although their hearts speak volumes. Questions and doubts battle through their minds as they seek the courage to speak or the grace to not. Good luck to all of you!

Sincerely,
Tara Nielson
Proud birthmother

Tara Nielson is twenty-eight years old and birthmother to Thomas, who was born February 13, 2000. Tara and Thomas's birthfather, Chad, have been together for ten years, and happily married for three years. They are grateful for, and enjoy, a fully open adoption with Thomas's adoptive family, seeing each other as much as schedules allow. Tara remains active in adoption by speaking at workshops for prospective adoptive parents and mentoring new birthparents. She works as a registered nurse in oncology and palliative care and volunteers as a leader with Girl Guides of Canada. She and Chad live in Red Deer, Alberta. They are expecting their second baby in December 2008.

Appendix A

Entrustment Ceremony for Diana Emily Rose
October 24, 1999

MINISTER: "WE COME together today to celebrate the birth and future life of this child, Diana Emily Rose. May all of you who have come on this joyous occasion be blessed. We are honoured to share with two families the role each plays in Diana's life and to acknowledge the entrustment of her by her birthmother, Artrina, to Dave, Debbie, and Daniel, who are to be her parents and brother. Today is a day of dedication, a day of welcome and of recognition.

"Let us pray.

"God in heaven, we thank you for your compassion in times of change and transition. In the midst of our pains and joys, we gather today to give you thanks for this gift of new life. We thank you for this child's birthmother, Artrina, through whom in your infinite wisdom [you] brought Diana into this world. We give thanks for the relationship of trust and mutual love for this child that has created a new family for Debbie, Dave, and Daniel. Guide them all in the days ahead as their lives move forward and as Diana grows in their loving care. Amen."

[Minister gestures to rose]

"Let us reflect on this beautiful rose, a symbol of life unfolding. As a flower grows, so do we. Whether the rose develops and blooms to its full glory depends on the nurture it receives.

No flower grows alone, apart from sunshine and rain, apart from the soil in which it lives. So too, no child grows alone."

Artrina's thoughts: "When my sister gave me the article, I had my doubts. But from the first moment I spoke to you, I knew you were the ones to raise my child. This has been one of the most difficult decisions of my life. Never have I been so torn up inside. I trust in you, Debbie, Dave, and Daniel, to bring up Diana in a good loving home. I've seen how you raised your son and am sure you will treat Diana as your own child. The day she was born was one of the hardest days of my life. As I held her in my arms, I knew I had made the right decision. Debbie, I believe with my whole heart that you will love and care for Diana so no harm will come to her. Finding that article was one of the luckiest days of my life. I feel as though someone was watching and that they now watch over our child. I have never doubted in my mind that you were the family for my child, and I'm sure I'll be even more positive as the years go by. Thank you for allowing me to be part of her life as well as yours. I will never forget the way you supported me and will always be thankful."

Dave and Debbie's thoughts: "Artrina — this day and always, we acknowledge your precious gift of Diana to our family. We promise that we will love, nurture, and protect her all of our lives. We will share with her all we have to give and surround her with family and friends who love her as we do.

"We promise to provide her with opportunities to grow and learn and make choices in her life, while always supporting her.

"Our wish for Diana is as ours for you: to have a full, happy, and healthy life, filled with loving relationships and meaningful goals. Daniel is already showing a great love for Diana and wants to be the best big brother ever. Together, we promise to be honest about her beginnings so that in doing so, she will never doubt how much she is loved by us all."

Minister: "There are three candles before us — one representing Artrina, one Diana, and the third, her new family. These candles symbolize the new light and life that began to shine on September 14, 1999, when Diana was born.

"It is fitting, then, that every year on her birthday, these candles should be lit to remember the greatest gift of all — the gift of Diana Emily Rose.

[Artrina then lights Diana's candle, and from Diana's candle lights the family candle]

[Artrina holds Diana now]

Minister: "Let us pray.

"Loving God, in whom is heaven, enfold these families in your grace. Send forth your abundant blessing on this child who is made in your image. We pray that she will have the best home possible: one filled with faith, hope, and deep love.

"As Artrina entrusts Diana's care to Debbie, Dave, and Daniel, may she have confidence and peace in her decision. Bestow upon Diana's new family your strength and ever present guidance in the days and years ahead.

"Watch over them all and protect this child forever and ever. Amen."

[Artrina then places Diana in Debbie's arms]

Glossary of Adoption Terms Used in Canada

Adoptee — Person who was adopted.

Adoption — The legal transfer of all parental rights and obligations to another person or couple.

Birth family — Those who share a child's genetic heritage.

Birthmother/father/parent — The birthmother, or biological mother, is the woman giving birth to a child who is subsequently placed for adoption. Avoid terms "real" or "natural"; these imply the existence of an "unreal" or "unnatural" mother. Some advocates also use "first mother."

Closed adoption — An adoption in which birth and adoptive families have no contact and know only non-identifying information about each other.

Constellation — A term coined by Professor Michael Grand to describe the groups of people involved in an adoption: primarily the birth family, adoptive family, and adoptee, but also other parties, adoption professionals, and foster families. (The more limited term *triad* refers to just the first three.)

Disclosure — In the field of adoption search and reunion, the release of government files of previously confidential information. A disclosure veto is a notice held on file that blocks release of identifying information.

Domestic adoption — Adoption of a child living in the same country as the adoptive parent(s).

Direct placement — When the birthparents of a child find a family and place their child directly with that family. A home study and approval of the adoptive family is still required.

Entrustment ceremony — A ritual where the parental role is transferred from the birthparents to the adoptive parents. Birthparents entrust the life of their child to the adoptive parents, often by physically placing the child in the adoptive parents' arms.

Fetal Alcohol Effect (FAE) — A disorder associated with cognitive and behavioural difficulties in children whose birthmother drank alcohol while pregnant.

Fetal Alcohol Syndrome (FAS) — Birth defects and serious lifelong mental and emotional difficulties that are a result of a child's prenatal exposure to alcohol.

Finalization — The last legal step in the adoption process, involving a court hearing, in which an adoptive parent becomes a child's legal parent.

Foster adoption — A foster placement intended to result in adoption, if and when the child becomes legally free for adoption.

Foster children — Children placed in the government's legal custody because their birth-parents were deemed abusive, neglectful, or otherwise unable to care for them.

Guardianship — A person who is legally responsible for a child. In kinship care, guardianship may serve as an alternative to adoption, when the child's relative assumes a parental role but prefers not to adopt. Guardianship is subject to ongoing supervision by the court and ends by court order or when the child reaches the age of majority.

Hague Convention — The Hague Convention on Protection of Children and Co-operation in Respect of Intercountry Adoption, inaugurated in 1993, is an international treaty that set the framework for the adoption of children between countries. The aim is to protect the best interests of adopted children and prevent abuses. The Convention standardizes procedures between the adoption authority in the child's country of origin and the corresponding authority in the receiving country. Each country that has ratified the Convention designates a central authority to regulate requests for intercountry adoption and accredit adoption agencies. In Canada each province has its own central authority responsible for adoption.

Home study — Comprehensive professional assessment of a prospective parent's suitability to adopt, including interviews by a social worker, summary of education, medical history, and police checks. Home studies must be updated annually and are provided by public agencies at no cost to the applicants. There is a cost to having a home study prepared by a private agency or individual.

Licensed adoption agency — An agency to whom the provincial adoption ministry has granted a licence to place children for adoption in the province and to manage the adoption process until finalization. The process of licensing is governed by provincial regulations. Ontario is the only province allowing individuals to be licensed and uses the term *licensee* to mean either a licensed person or a licensed agency.

Open adoption — An adoption that involves some direct contact between the birth and adoptive families, ranging from exchanging non-identifying information through an intermediary (semi-open) to a full ongoing relationship with visits and regular interaction (open). The open adoption agreement may be verbal or written, but it is not legally binding.

Permanency — Arrangement that assures lasting care and parenting of a child and eliminates the need for further moves.

Placement — Act of physically placing a child in a foster or prospective adoptive home.

Post-adoption services — Services provided after adoption finalization to birth families, adoptive families, and adoptees by a public agency, private therapist, or community organization. These services may consist of subsidies, respite care, counselling, daycare, medical equipment, support groups, and peer support programs.

Private adoption — An adoption arranged by a privately funded licensed adoption agency. All private adoption is regulated by the provincial ministry responsible for adoptions. Ministries license individuals and agencies to place children privately, approve the social workers to conduct home studies, and monitor the performance of licensees and social workers. In some provinces, such as British Columbia, Manitoba, and Ontario, agencies are licensed to placed children not only from the province but also from abroad (international adoption).

Private agency — Non-government adoption agency licensed by the province the agency operates in. Private agencies charge fees for their services.

Public adoption — An adoption arranged through a provincial ministry or agency funded by the government. Government-funded agencies usually provide services at no cost.

Relinquishment —The legally binding process by which birthparents voluntarily surrender rights to parent their children. This is not a preferred term when placing a child for adoption. Better is "birthparents choose adoption" or "birthparents make an adoption plan for their child."

Respite care — Temporary care provided for a child in order to give parents relief from their responsibilities as caregivers.

Special needs — Conditions in a child, ranging in severity, that are particularly challenging to adoptive parents; can include physical, emotional, and behavioural disorders.

Subsidy (adoption) — Government benefit to offset the costs of adopting and raising a special-needs child. The benefit may take the form of one-time or monthly payments, medical aid, and/or post-adoption services. In Canada, parents adopting children with special needs may get a payment to defray unusual expenses, such as medical and dental expenses, counselling services and therapy not covered by health insurance, or social workers for advice and respite care. Amounts and types of subsidies vary by province.

Waiting children — Children who are legally free for adoption and waiting to be adopted. They are in the care of the public child welfare system and cannot return to their birth families. According to the May 2002 "Report Card on Adoption" by the Adoption Council of Canada, there are more than 66,000 Canadian children in foster care. About 22,000 are permanent wards of the provincial governments and await adoption, but fewer than 1,700 of them are adopted annually across the country.

These terms compiled with material from North America Council of Adoptable Children and the Adoption Council of Canada. For a more comprehensive list, visit their websites: www.nacac.org and www.adoption.ca.

Canadian Adoption Organizations, Websites, and Resources

Adoption Council of Canada
Tel: (613) 235-0344
www.adoption.ca

Adoption Council of Ontario
Tel: (416) 482-0021
aco@adoption.ca

Family Helper
Robin Hilborn, Editor
Southampton
helper@familyhelper.net

North American Council on Adoptable Children (NACAC)
Joe Kroll, Executive Director
www.nacac.org

Canada's Waiting Kids
Tel: 1-888-542-3678 (toll-free)
www.canadaswaitingkids.ca

AdoptOntario
www.adoptontario.ca

Dave Thomas Foundation for Adoption
www.davethomasfoundcation.ca

Parentbooks
Tel: (416) 537-9499
www.parentbooks.ca
201 Harbord Street
Toronto ON, Canada
M5S 1H6

Provincial Adoption Agencies and Government Links

ALBERTA

Adoption By Choice
Calgary and Edmonton offices
Tel: 1–800–570–2835 (toll-free)
www.adoptionbychoice.ca

Alberta Children and Youth Services
www.child.alberta.ca

Catholic Social Services
Edmonton
Tel: (780) 701–9486
Red Deer
Tel: (403) 347–8844

BRITISH COLUMBIA

Choices Adoption and Counseling Services
Victoria
Tel: 1-888-479-9811 (toll-free)
CHOICES@choicesadoption.ca

Family Services of Greater Vancouver
Vancouver
Tel: (604) 736-7613
Adoptionservices@fsgv.ca

Hope Services
Abbotsford
Tel: 1-800-916-4673 (toll-free)
adoption@shaw.ca

Sunrise Adoption Centre
North Vancouver
Tel: 1-888-984-2488 (toll-free)
dchalke@sunriseadoption.ca

The Adoption Center
Kelowna
Tel: 1-800-935-4237 (toll-free)
adoption@kcr.ca

Ministry of Children and Family Development
www.mcf.gov.bc.ca/adoption

MANITOBA

Manitoba Family Services and Housing
Winnipeg Child and Family Services
csd@gov.mb.ca

Adoption Options
sgr@adoptionoptions.mb.ca

NEW BRUNSWICK

Government of New Brunswick
www.gnb.ca

NEWFOUNDLAND AND LABRADOR

Government of Newfoundland
www.gov.nf.ca/health/matterofhealth/adoptions

NORTHWEST TERRITORIES
Northwest Territories Health and Social Services
www.hlthss.gov.nt.ca

NOVA SCOTIA

Home of the Guardian Angel
Tel: (902) 422-7964
hga@nsaliantzinc.cz

Community Services
www.gov.ns.ca/coms/families/adoption

ONTARIO

Adoption Agency and Counselling Service
Markham
Tel: (905) 475-3386

Adoption Resource and Counselling Services (ARCS)
Kingston
Tel: (613) 542-0275

Beginnings Counselling and Adoption Services of Ontario
Hamilton
Tel: (905) 528-6665
info@beginnings.ca

Children's Resource and Consultation Centre of Ontario
Toronto
Tel: (416) 923-7771
mjblug@total.net

Kids Link International Adoption Agency
St. Anne Adoption Centre
Cambridge
Tel: (519) 623-5437
admin@kids-link.ca
admin@stanneadoption.org

The Children's Bridge
Nepean
Tel: (613) 226-2112
www.childrensbridge.com

Ministry of Children and Youth Services
www.children.gov.on.ca

PRINCE EDWARD ISLAND

Social Services
www.gov.pei.ca/infopei

QUEBEC

Adoption internationale inc.
Westmount
Tel: (514) 933-4453

Les enfants du Mandé: L'agence d'adoption internationale Québec-Afrique
Boucherville
Tel: (450) 641-4682
infomali@enfantsdumande.org

Alliance des families du Quebec
Laval
Tel: (450) 689-4438
adoptquebec@yahoo.ca

Ministry of Social Services
Leceta Chisholm Guibault
Tel: (613) 235-0344
www.adoption.gouv.qc.da

SASKATCHEWAN

Saskatchewan Social Services
www.cr.gov.sk.ca/adoption

Adoption Support Centre of Saskatchewan
Adoption.support@sasktel.net
www.adoptionsask.org

Adoption Books, Magazines, and Newsletters

What Is Adoption?
Rita McDowall and Sofie Stergianis
Wisdom Press, 2006
ISBN-10: 0973816600
Helping non-adopted children understand adoption.

The Open Adoption Experience: Complete Guide for Adoptive and Birth Families
Lois Ruskai Melina and Sharon Kaplan Roszia
New York: Harper Collins, 1993
ISBN-10: 0-06-096957-1
Excellent introduction to the risks and rewards of open adoption.

Making Sense of Adoption: A Parent's Guide
Lois Ruskai Melina
New York: Harper & Row Publishers, 1989

ISBN-10: 0-06-055138-0
Adoption experts connect the dots and offers useful tips on how to handle everything your children may throw at you.

Toddler Adoption: The Weaver's Craft
Mary Hopkins-Best
Indiana: Perspective Press, 1998
ISBN-10:0944934218
Parenting a child who arrives older than infancy but younger than kindergarten age. Support and practical tools for transitioning and promoting attachment.

Adoptive Parents' Guide to the Special Needs Child
Robin Hilborn
www.familyhelper.net
Attachment disorder, Attention Deficit hyperactive Disorder, Fetal Alcohol Syndrome, effects of institutional care, learning disabilities, and sensory integration dysfunction.

Recognizing and Managing Children With Fetal Alcohol Syndrome/Fetal Alcohol Effect: A Guidebook
Brenda McCreight
www.theadoptioncounselor.com
British Columbia adoptive parent and social worker offers advice on dealing with children with FAS/E; medical, historical, and social aspects.

Tell Me About the Night I Was Born
Jamie Lee Curtis
New York: Harper Collins, 1996
ISBN–10: 006024528X
Bedtime story by the star of *Halloween* and *A Fish Called Wanda*.

How It Feels to Be Adopted
Jill Kremetz
New York: Knopf, 1982
ISBN-10: 0394758536
Adopted children share their experiences.

Post Adoption Blues
Karen J. Foli and John R. Thompson
St. Martin's Press, 2004
ISBN-10: 1579548660
Offers parents the understanding, support, and concrete solutions they need to overcome the post–adoption blues.

Secret Thoughts of an Adoptive Mother
Jana Woloff
Vista Communications, 1997
ISBN-10: 0967214319

Real Parents, Real Children
Holly Van Guldan
Crossroad Pub Co., 1993
ISBN-10: 0824515145

Arms Wide Open: An Inside to Open Adoption
Jane Waters
ISBN-10: 1420878549

Raising Adopted Children
Lois Ruskai Melina

HarperCollins Publishers Inc., 1998
ISBN-10: 0060957174

Twenty Things Adopted Kids Wish Their Adoptive Parents Knew
Sherry Eldridge
Dell Publishing, 1999
ISBN-10: 044050838X

Adopting the Hurt Child: Hope for Families
Gregory C. Keck
Pinon Press, 1995
ISBN-10: 1576830942

Dear Birthmother
Kathleen Silber, Phylis Speedlin
Corona Publishing Co., 1982
ISBN-10: 0931722209

Children of Open Adoption and Their Families
Kathleen Silber, Patricia Martinez Dorner
Corona Publishing Co., 1989
ISBN-10: 0931722780

Gone to An Aunt's: Remembering Canada's Homes for Unwed Mothers
Anne Petrie
McClelland & Stewart, 1998
ISBN-10: 0771069715

Yesterday They Took My Baby: True Stories of Adoption
Ben Wicks
Random House UK Ltd., 1993
ISBN-10: 041345514

Adoption Helper
www.familyhelper.net
Advice and information on how to adopt in Canada and overseas.

Adoption Round-up
Journal published by the Adoption Council of Ontario.

Post-Adoption Helper
Newsletter covering what you need to know after you've adopted.

For more comprehensive listings of adoption-related books, refer to Parentbooks and websites noted in this resources section.

The Photographers

Rebecca Craigie
Victoria, British Columbia
rebeccajane76@yahoo.ca

Angela Colwell, Living Waters Photography
Trail, British Columbia
www.living-waters.ca
Tel: (250) 364-2833

Jill Shantz, CPAJ, Shantz Photography
St. Albert, Alberta
www.jshantzphoto.com

Shelley Weber, As I See It Photography
Calgary, Alberta
www.asiseeitphotography.ca
Echo21@shaw.ca

George Fraser, Image Studios
Cold Lake, Alberta
www.imagestudios.com

Tobias Beharrell, Zane Media
Winnipeg, Manitoba
www.zanemedia.com
tobias@zanemedica.com
Tel: (204) 694-6233

Liz Lott, Snapdragon Photography
North Bay, Ontario
snapdragon@thot.net
www.lizlott.com

Kirsten White
Toronto, Ontario
www.whitestudio.ca
kir.white@gmail.com

Chris Hardy, Zoom-in Photography
Oakville, Ontario
chrishardy@cogeco.ca

Daniel St. Louis
Moncton, New Brunswick
www.danielst.louis.com
photoart@danielst.louis.com
Tel: (506) 855-1200

Anne Kmetyko, Anne Kmetyko Photography
Montreal, Quebec
www.annkmetyko.com

Julian Katz, Julian Katz Photography
Guelph, Ontario
www.juliankatz.com

And special thanks to Bill Hewitt, whose expert eye and organzational skills brought all the imagery together for the book. Bill is also credited with the fine digital restorations of the original photographs of Jeff Healey.

Bill Hewitt, C.P.S. Ink Works
Oakville, Ontario
www. cpsinkworks.com
Tel: (905) 844-6634

Acknowledgements

I FIRST MUST acknowledge that without Artrina Heinbecker, Diana's birthmother, I would not have known the miracle of adoption. Our relationship, which has at its nucleus the most extraordinary girl, Diana, is precious to our family. We continue the journey together.

To the wonderful families who shared their stories, all unique and special in their own right, and who welcomed me into their lives and homes — thank you. Now the readers of this book will also benefit from your wisdom and insights into adoption. I thank you for your time, your enthusiasm, and your willingness to open your hearts to us all.

To the adoption professionals, who know the subject so thoroughly by working in it for decades and often by experiencing it personally, thank you for providing a window into policies, practices, and your hopes for the future. If we are able to be true advocates for children, we must continue to work together towards the goal of finding loving permanent homes for every child.

Thanks to the photographers who so enthusiastically joined me on this journey, some-times under less than ideal circumstances, but always with patience, understanding, and integrity. Your photography brought beautiful images to the conversations — an invaluable element in portraying these extraordinary families and professionals. Special thanks to Liz Lott, who provided the beautiful front and back cover photographs, and for going the extra mile and working so hard for the project.

To Brian Henry, for introducing me to the world of writing and for teaching me the fundamentals of successfully navigating the obstacle course that is book publishing.

To Dr. David Posen, who has been a mentor to me in so many ways and who believed that I could achieve my dream. Your practical wisdom and guidance in the last fifteen years has been, and continues to be, invaluable.

To Sally Keefe Cohen, without whom this book might have remained unwritten. Thank you, Sally, for your expertise, impeccable judgment, patience, and unique ability to somehow lower my blood pressure just by listening. I also appreciate that you even laughed at my sometimes questionable sense of humour. Your steady nature kept me afloat when I thought I might sink.

To Peter Perkovic and Judy Knox, whose chance meeting with me at an antique store in 2004 turned into a long conversation about personal adoption experiences, and whose connection became a great source of inspiration.

To Lorraine, Kelly x 2, Catherine, Gail, Elli, Sharon, Diane, and Lori, thanks for cheering me on and having faith in me, even when you might think me a little crazy.

To my dear friend Tania Honan, thanks for your unfailing support, countless cups of tea, and meetings in parking lots as we exchanged my writings. Thank you for turning the scrawl into a legible manuscript, but most of all for your steadfast friendship. I appreciate also the willingness of Lisa Frauley to jump into the fray at the end and help with the manuscript. Your experience as an adoptive mother of two children added welcome dimension to my ideas.

To my sister, Kathy — what can I say? You have always been there for me, and this journey has been no exception. I can't imagine not being able to speak to you at the drop of a hat and hear your calm encouragement when I need it. Thank you for being my best friend, confidante, and shoulder to lean on.

To my niece, Meghan, thank you for lighting up my life with your radiance inside and out; to my nephew, Chris for staying sweet, jellybeans or not.

To my family: my husband, David, for realizing this book, however long and arduous the process, has meant so much to me; our cherished son, Daniel, who at five asked to have a sister and is still learning what that means; and of course to Diana, for enriching our lives beyond measure.

Finally, to my father, Bruce Witherspoon, who by the time we lost him, thirty-three years ago had given me a lifetime full of wisdom. Thank you for teaching me the importance of being true to myself, persevering in matters of passion, embracing life, and staying the course. Your unfailing confidence in my potential gave me the courage to pursue this dream. I hear your voice still, and it forever guides, comforts, and encourages me.

Marquis Book Printing Inc.

Québec, Canada
2008